the Dublin Review

number three | SUMMER 2001

EDITOR: BRENDAN BARRINGTON

ISBN 1 901866 86 6
ISSN 1393-998X

The Dublin Review, number three (Summer 2001). Design by Atelier (David Smith). Printed by Betaprint, Baldoyle, Dublin.

The Dublin Review is published quarterly. Editorial and business correspondence to P.O. Box 7948, Dublin 1. Unsolicited material should take the form of typescript only and should be accompanied by a self-addressed stamped envelope or, if coming from outside the Republic of Ireland, a self-addressed envelope with International Reply coupons. The Dublin Review assumes no responsibility for such material.

SUBSCRIPTIONS: £20 per year (Ireland and Great Britain), £30 / $45 per year (rest of world). Institutions add £10 / $15. To subscribe please send address and cheque or Visa/MC data to P.O. Box 7948, Dublin 1.

TRADE SALES: The Dublin Review is distributed to the trade by Gill & Macmillan Distribution, Hume Avenue, Park West, Dublin 12. Sales representation: Robert Towers, 2 The Crescent, Monkstown, Co. Dublin, tel 01 2806532, fax 01 2806020 (Ireland); Andrew Russell, 73 St Dunstan's Road, London W6 8RE, tel 0208 7481870, fax 0208 7486614 (Britain).

The Dublin Review is published with financial assistance from An Chomhairle Ealaíon / The Arts Council of Ireland.

the arts
council
an chomhairle
ealaíon
50+

Contents | *number three* | SUMMER 2001

The parting of the ways

RUTH PADEL

It is the winter solstice in Orissa. St Lucy's Day, at the end of the second millennium. What did St Lucy do, to get the darkest day? But this is India, and the afternoon light is deciduous winter dapple on the head and back of a large male tiger, waking from a sexy doze in a dry hill-forest.

Every tiger face has two white patches winging up like two higher bigger eyes above the surprisingly small, kohl-rimmed circles of the real eyes. Stripe patterns in these white patches vary, and this tiger is asymmetrical. Over the right eye, a blurred little black triangle with three concentric crescent moons above. Over the left, an eyebrow like a worm of black flame. His massy lurid head is rolled against the white-ruffed neck of a tigress.

Daytime is sleep time for tigers but these ones have hardly slept for three days and nights. December is peak of the mating season. He has been with his tigress non-stop all these hours, two days and two nights. They've fucked eight times in half an hour, sometimes. A hundred times a day. When he gets tired she growls, squirms, backs up to him, and gets him back on course. They haven't eaten, have barely slept. Par for the course, for the king and queen of the jungle. That's why trade in tiger aphrodisiacs is so big.

In Taoism, the tiger's breath creates the wind and dragon's breath creates the clouds. When they get together, they make rain, the stuff of life. After years of searching and a thousand days of disciplined instruction, the founder of Taoism, Chang Tao-Ling, ascended into heaven and discovered the tiger-dragon elixir of immortality. The recipe is secret but Chang is always depicted riding a tiger, which gives a strong hint that tigers are the vehicle of eternal life.

That's the thing. That's why tiger-bone pills are meant to help your rheumatism, why wine made from them is the elixir of youth. In a Taiwan chemist's window today you'll see a tiger's skull advertising tiger medicines, or pick-me-up tonics made from tiger whiskers, to be sold undercover within. There is nothing to say, even in Chinese, that this is the skull of a tiger. But those who need it, or think they need it, know. Next door, they are selling pills made from ground-up tigers' eyes, to cure cataracts and convulsions.

But most of all, there's sex. Sex reminds you of eternal life, doesn't it? Seems like it, at the time. So tiger-penis soup sells at $400 a bowl, and Chinese businessmen, newspaper moguls, music entrepreneurs and politicians tuck in before a night on the town. Safer, more traditional, more glamorous than blue pills called Viagra. More personal and mythic; more a state of mind. You are borrowing the body of your dreams, robing yourself in royal, ferocious, omnivalent loins. Tiger penises, stretched-out, stiff and smoky orange, untidy salami with shrunken kidneys attached like plum vine tomatoes to their stem, are on sale this minute, illegal and expensive, in the secret shopping malls of Harbin.

In the sixties, the Chinese government tried to wipe the tiger out as an agricultural pest, harmful to pastoral progress. They did a fine job. If evolutionary speculation is right, the Chinese tiger was the species from which all other tigrine races originally diverged, the ancestral *Felis Paleosinesis*. Mao's government made war on three thousand Chinese tigers, who have followed their ancestor into extinction. By dying, they created a dead-tiger mountain, plus a unique chance to expand the sale of traditional tiger products.

Tigers began to pay a heavy price for their ancestors' hold on human fantasies. Tigers are strong: more than a fifth of the world's human population believes their ground-up bones are strong enough to cure lower-back pain and strengthen human muscle. For one, two, maybe even four thousand years, tiger bones have been an essential part of a traditional medical-care system that was – and still is – the one thing many people turn to in their struggle against every form of pain. Most grown–up Western broadsheets still run horoscopes, and many have hotlines these days too; in China, tiger blood is a strengthening tonic, tiger tail cures skin disease, tiger whiskers cure toothache. Meanwhile in

India, tiger fat has always been used against leprosy; and ground-up tiger claws are a sedative in Laos. The fact that the calcium in tiger bone is no different from the calcium in leopard, penguin, pig or human bone is neither here nor there. The magic of your own history dies hard.

So many parts of this wonderful dangerous wild body, for the many places and parts where the tame, soft, frightened human body can hurt and fail. The humerus, the upper front leg bone, is supposed to be the most powerful tiger bone, though with the dwindling of supply all parts of the skeleton are used today. Traditional Chinese medics attribute to it the special properties of Acrid, Sweet and Warm. All these, they say, enter the bloodstream through the liver and kidney. Tiger bone has a Latin name too (*Os Tigris*), so it must work. It is toasted or baked in oil or vinegar, mixed with anti-inflammatory medicinal plants, then ground up and blended in individually prepared remedies. Or else, depending on who's bought the illegal bones, it is manufactured as patent medicine, as a powder or pill. A sweet round tabby tiger head, mustard and soot, stares straight at you with rich brown eyes from the lid of a little white box saying 'Analgesic Plaster'. Illegal; but you find them anywhere Chinese traditional medicine is sold, from Shen Zhen in China to London to Belgium, if you know where to look. As you read this today, somebody somewhere is selling some to a man in pain.

By the middle of the 1980s, the tiger-bone stockpile was dwindling, but demand for tiger products was growing. When tigers became news as an endangered species, the Chinese government revoked its extermination policy,. But by now tiger medicine had an established modern market. In China, Taiwan, Hong Kong, South Korea, the fact that it was now, exotically, both globally illegal and rare, meant that demand and price soared.

And as air rushes into the vacuum none of us in real life has ever seen, so poachers from all tiger countries rushed into the jungle – or, in Siberia, into pine forests and snow – and out again to the city, above all New Delhi, to meet the raging demand for tiger parts. In one raid in Delhi in 1993, police found

850lbs of tiger bones, what was left of forty-two tigers. Between 1991 and 1994 in India alone, they say, poachers killed and sold maybe a thousand tigers. A fifth, perhaps, of the current population.

Riding the tiger is living forever, having sex eternally and tirelessly as tigers do (or seem to – this tiger is very tired indeed) on their three-day benders. Tough on the tiger, but for a matter as important as your sex life something has to give.

China has executed seven people in five years for 'crimes against tigers', whatever that is in Chinese. But you can't stop men-about-town worrying about their potency, and shoring it up for the night with whatever the iconic dreams of their ancient culture say will do it best.

The male stands up and stretches. The light is buttery scatter round them both, falling through feathery trees on these redgold coats that haven't been apart from each other all these days and nights. Lazily, he rears up on his hind legs, unsheaths those scary claws from the cream-coloured, tick- and leech-filled fur of his huge front feet, and stretches, all eight foot of him, to scratch a tree. His belly and back arch in like a swag of washing. He is making his mark.

He is five years old, in his prime. His coat is heavy and hot. He drops down and sniffs the tree where the tigress sprayed a few hours ago, and his upper lip draws back in a special tiger grimace, greeting the smell from which he gets his all-important news: the age, sex, size, and physical condition – maybe even the emotional condition, who knows? – of another tiger.

Tigers are too heavily armed to meet often. Like nuclear powers, they depend on peaceful co-existence with their only peers, each other. Conventions as hierarchic and byzantine as the protocols of NATO govern their meetings. They have worked out a silent gossip of scent-marking, a careful code for avoiding combat. The blend of urine and anal-gland secretions keeps everyone out of trouble. The males reverse their costly penises, pointing them back between their gold-and-white hind legs to shoot out jets that hit the spot exactly. These spray-marks are the centre of their social life, their dinner jacket, shopfront, poste restante: tangy hieroglyphs of guarded self-advertisement. Females just squirt the rock or bush behind them with a pyramid of quick drizzle.

Male and female almost never meet, except in these three-day bouts of sex. Now the sex, and all that goes with it, is nearly over.

Tigers are wary, solitary and emotional. The grammar of their socializing has been catalogued in German for human beings. Tiger behaviour: a Wagner opera. This tiger doesn't know, and doesn't care, but the muscles of his upper lip have just performed the spasm known as *flehmen* in the tiger-observation trade. He has sucked in a scent through two holes in his palate, interpreting the range of fragrance of another tiger's pee like a wine snob or scent-taster for Armani, upper lip so wrinkled back above his teeth that a deep furrow runs the length of his nose. Here he stays a moment, savouring the smell with a set of nerve cells called, by tiger ethologists, his Jacobson's organ.

His tail brushes against the tigress. She turns her massive head and stares at him.

Impassive, we would say. There is no emotion written on her face for us to read. But what does he see? This is tiger love. They lay for an hour earlier, with her body half in half out of bright green water weed, her paws resting over his as he lay splayed and exhausted on the ground, her head against his pale gold and white chest. For the hours of thirty-six football matches, if you played them back to back, they have been touching each other, making each other's body their own medium of breathing.

When not on the job they have been playing, rubbing against each other, rolling over and over, entwined all this time, not ever not touching each other, in and out of the water. Sometimes she swipes at him, a claws-out forehand serve that could kill a chital or a sambur if its head got in the way; and he ducks back out of the way, play-snarling. Or is it play? They have to be careful of each other, even in love. In sex she has to turn her back on him, and he takes her by the scruff of the neck, which for any other animal would be the death grip, perfected over his five years of life. If he hadn't learnt it, he'd have gone under. Like the robin in the garden, he has to kill to live.

Bodies don't show bliss in the same way and tigers cannot purr. The roars and growls and grunts and chirrupings of these two have rung through this part of the forest continuously for three nights and days. Today's biologists classify a tiger as *Panthera Tigris*. Once they classed it with true cats in the genus *Felis*, but after a luminary called Owen studied the hyoid bone of the cat larynx they heaved the tiger into the genus *Panthera*, along with the lion, leopard and jaguar. In cats, the hyoid bone is held close to the skull by a series of short bones joined end to end. In lions, leopards, jaguars and tigers, this series of bones is imperfectly ossified. Instead, you find a long elastic ligament, a flexible gristly attachment of jaw to larynx, which lets the larynx move more. That is what gets you the roar.

But though tigers have the wrong sort of throat-bones for purring, they have a wide repertoire of little sounds, like the breathy puffy panting called *prusten*, which says you're in, you're the business, I love you – for now. Mother tigers do birdlike chirrups to young cubs. And all tigers do an odd gruff hiccough called *pooking* (don't ask) to advertise their presence and ward off those tricky, dangerous meetings with other tigers.

Her whiskers twitch. One ear rotates back, and forward. A bulbul calls comically and urgently in the tree above. The forest is very still. He turns to rub his ruff and chin lazily against her neck. For a moment no birds call at all. You can imagine them holding their varied breaths. Maybe tonight we'll get some real sleep, not be kept awake by the yowls and roars and growls and snarls and moans of tiger paradise.

Then the spell breaks, the birds re-start their evening calling, a langur, the large grey monkey of the Indian forest, tries a soft, far-off interrogative whoo-op, whoo-op.

The tigress has been lying against a rock; now she gets slowly to her feet. Was there a signal? Not that anyone outside would tell. She is as tall as he is but paler; her stripes are wider apart; she is less massed and heavy. The two walk slowly, ruff to ruff, suede shoulder to suede shoulder, down to the rubbery brown pool. Tigers love water. They never lie far from it if they can help it. Though they haven't eaten together, they have had to drink. Now they move down, turn round like two combine harvesters in a parking lot, and get in backwards. It looks clumsy and a bit bathetic; these two huge beauties suddenly turning into overweight wussy businessmen too scared to dive, backing into a chilly pool. Tigers don't care. They like to keep their faces and whiskers dry.

They stink, these two, head to arse to toe, of sex and blood and rotting teeth and rolled-in urine. You'd perform a spot of *flehmen* yourself if you got close. But all smells disappear as they slip into the bloodwarm pool and swim together side by side. All you can see are two heads in the water in parallel, calm as masks. They play a little in the lapping light, which is now nearly horizontal, picking up their ripples as long black wrinkles, liquid rubber bands skimmering over the surface of the pool.

Then, in a split second, the tigress puts a stop to all their synchronized movement. She is suddenly a tiger on her own. She touches her face against his, turns her head towards the farther bank, and swims slowly away. He stays in the centre, watching. She climbs out, her seven-foot body staggering and ungainly a moment on the bank till she gets her balance back. Brown water drops fall from her belly like cappuccino on dry mud and split-endy jungle grass. She pauses, her body en route away from him, turning only her head back towards the water.

All the markings on her wide ruffed face, its circlet yellow eyes meeting his as he watches her, head only visible from the pool, are perfectly symmetrical. The soft kohl outline round her rose-brown nose. Two stark black hammer-and-sickle curlicues in the white wings above her eyes. Barber's-pole black stripes, fanning out toward the ears.

Tigers spread away from each other very carefully in a forest. Each one alone establishes a territory they get to know so intimately they could walk it blind and never break a twig or roll a stone. They don't want domination, just space in which to find enough food and – when it comes round – sex. When prey and cover are scarce, tigers live farther apart from each other than they do in thick jungle frothing with several kinds of deer, with peacock – this is the Indian jungle, this is where peacocks come from, where they live wild – and scuffly herds of grey-black pig.

But male and female tigers have dramatically different ideas about territory. A female holds a small territory, enough to feed herself and her cubs. This tigress is about to start a demanding two-year job, the basic unit of tiger civilization: a single mother rearing cubs, devotedly teaching them, even when they are as tall as she is, to survive, listen, look, wait, and kill. A male holds a much bigger area, a super-territory which covers those of several females, if he's lucky. It might have other transient younger males in it too from time to time, who when they smell his traces will seek him out and challenge him if they are feeling strong; and stop dead as if at a customs post when the smell of his spray-mark hits them, and head in the other direction, if they're not.

The tigress turns her head away and walks on into the forest. All he sees of her are the two mad white dots, the target centres on the round black backs of tiger ears. Then she's gone, carrying his three days of semen back to the depths of her territory, into the dark.

The tiger pushes deeper away into the water, still keeping his head up and whiskers dry, through a chain of pools to another part of the forest, where he's used to hunting alone. Where the sambur and wild boar drink at dusk.

Light rain begins to fall on the calming surface of the empty pool. Small animals, voles, frogs, chipmunks, breathe differently now the gods have left the drinking hole. Humbler, shyer life comes back to normal round the edges of flattened grass.

Mister Impersonality himself

HARRY CLIFTON

In the nineteen-seventies, I heard Denis Donoghue read from a lectern on the Belfield campus of University College Dublin, to an amphitheatre of first-year literature students. I was one of those students. The text in question was 'Sunday Morning', Wallace Stevens's great meditation on the passing away of Christian belief and its replacement by the lonely self-sufficiencies of our own day.

> She says, "I am content when wakened birds,
> Before they fly, test the reality
> Of misty fields, by their sweet questionings;
> But when the birds are gone, and their warm fields
> Return no more, where, then, is paradise?"

What that meant to the other listeners – the smokers at the back, the throwers of paper rockets – I do not know. But for me a door had opened, from the prison of the Irish school curriculum. There was land to the west, where the sun also rose. I did not know it at the time, but only a generation previously Denis Donoghue had discovered that land for himself, perhaps from the same inner necessity.

The university itself had just moved from its city-centre premises at Earlsfort Terrace to the new Belfield campus. Students filed through a war-zone of mud, craters and JCBs, on their way to and from lectures. A decade of construction was putting in place the shockproof functional edifice that is there today, all air and light, impersonal abstract space. It felt, even then, of a piece with the American New Critical ethos, a seminar of the pure intellect chaired by the ghost of Eliot, Mister Impersonality himself. Denis Donoghue, his representative on earth, or at least in the UCD of the seventies, could be seen stooping like a lepidopterist after some treasure from the university bookstacks of an afternoon, adding fresh elements to an endless argument with himself. He seemed to me then – and nothing in his new study of Eliot, *Words Alone*, does anything to change my mind – one of the happiest men alive.

That happiness, if *Words Alone* is anything to go by, seems traceable to his escape, as a young UCD lecturer at the start of the fifties, into the New Critical heaven of Tate and Ransom, Winters, Blackmur, Kenner, Brooks et al., with the papal figure of Eliot, whose own work as poet and critic lay at the centre of their debate, above and behind it all. A time, a climate characterized later by Robert Lowell as one of 'waiting for the next essay with the same excitement as for a new work of imagination'. It is hard to imagine Myles, or Brendan Behan, or indeed Patrick Kavanagh, the then representative figures of literary Dublin, with its special intensities and destructiveness, rushing at lunch-hour, as Donoghue describes himself doing, to buy the latest Eliot pamphlet – 'The Three Voices of Poetry' – just in at Hodges Figgis. Donoghue's excitement is palpable, as of a man who had found his America, his new-found land, and be damned to the Dublin begrudgers. One of these, it would seem, was the above-mentioned Kavanagh, himself an occasional lecturer in the UCD of the fifties. But of that more later.

Autobiography in the form of literary criticism: that is the signal from the dustjacket of *Words Alone*. In fact, the personal element, the insertion into the narrative of Denis Donoghue the bundle of accidents who sits down to breakfast, are few enough to begin with and dwindle altogether as the book progresses. Indirection, theoretical distancing to the point where the Self is eliminated, are the preferred methods. Yet there is a story in the depths of all the literary criticism, and its essence is the re-reading, by a mature man, of a book (in this case the *Collected Poems* of T.S. Eliot) he was once passionate about, perhaps too passionate about, in youth. By comparing the two readings, Donoghue gauges the state of his own beliefs where language and religion are concerned. If it is autobiography, it is so only in Eliot's sense of the word – an autobiography not of Self, but of Soul.

In the telling, it becomes a kind of love story, or the story of how an infatuation becomes love, the difference being that love, unlike infatuation, cultivates an ironic distance from what is beloved, without ceasing to love it. The achievement of that ironic distance vis-à-vis Eliot, the avoidance of unconscious identification, seems to have been a lifetime's labour for Donoghue. At the end of it, he can acknowledge the negative aspects of Eliot, even upbraid him for the elements in his work or personality that are hardest to take. The strange capacity for passing beyond friends, lovers and helpmeets who had outlived their usefulness – be it mythic or practical – on the way to the Divine Vision and the earthly married happiness of the last years. The hard-line religiosity that goes beyond a legitimate critique of the liberal mind to a hatred of life itself as a 'style of contentment'. The alleged anti-Semitism, evidence for and against which is set out even-handedly. 'No one', as Donoghue properly concludes, 'should feel an ethical superiority.'

So what are the traps for the infatuate of Eliot, especially if his name happens to be Denis Donoghue? As the chapters succeed one another, from 'Prufrock' through to the *Four Quartets*, three particular dangers present themselves. The first is Eliot's incantatory music, the way the lines interweave like a snake-charmer's spell, leaving the impression that something meaningful is being said, when in fact it is the hypnosis of the rhythm that is acting upon the reader:

> A woman drew her long black hair out tight
> And fiddled whisper music on those strings
> And bats with baby faces in the violet light
> Whistled, and beat their wings
> And crawled head downward down a blackened wall
> And upside down in air were towers

> Tolling reminiscent bells, that kept the hours
>
> And voices singing out of empty cisterns and exhausted wells.

That is magical, of course, but it would be hard to extract a meaning from it. And the problem (if it is a problem) recurs throughout Eliot's verse. On the other hand, meaningless though it may be in the conventional sense, it is not devoid of content. In fact, it is packed with emotional content, and is, as Donoghue puts it, 'the language of a feeling at its earliest stage of emergence'. What the feeling may be called – anxiety, disturbance, or something only those words in that particular order can express – is up to the reader to decide. Whatever it is, though, it is more than mere melody. Instead of meaning, a feeling is being communicated.

The second danger for the reader of Eliot is never quite knowing who is speaking in the poems. Is it Eliot himself, or a projection of Eliot in some exacerbated state of self-hatred (when he might call himself Prufrock) or anomie (when he might call himself Gerontion)? Or is it what Donoghue calls rather grandly the voice of God?

> Eyes I dare not meet in dreams
>
> In death's dream kingdom
>
> These do not appear;
>
> There the eyes are
>
> Sunlight on a broken column
>
> There, is a tree swinging
>
> And voices are
>
> In the wind's singing
>
> More distant and more solemn
>
> Than a fading star.

Not alone is it hard to hear the voice of a particular human being behind the disembodied eeriness of that extract from 'The Hollow Men', it is hard to relate the words in it to any particular object or situation beyond themselves either. They are, in fact, 'words alone', in the sense of being words without external reference, words alone with themselves inside a poem, not syntactically linked but following an emotional logic, in this case perhaps a sense of loss or fallenness. And the wrong way of reading Eliot – or the third danger, so to speak – is to mistake these 'words alone' for words in the ordinary sense with conventional meanings, when instead they are 'fading stars', light-traces arriving eons later from the black holes of unmapped emotional states. It is not Yeats's rather optimistic 'Words alone are certain good' that gives the book its title, but words as used by Robert Frost's protagonist, who got his 'native simile jarred' going through a door in the dark, to altered states of consciousness where

> People and things don't pair anymore
> With what they used to pair with before.

The echo of an incantation, the internal logic of feeling, a voice depersonalized to the voice of God. One remembers again those UCD lectures of the seventies, and the voice of God, which, then as now, threatens to become the voice of Denis Donoghue.

> Habermas has argued, in *The Philosophical Discourse of Modernity* (1987), that 'the paradigm of the philosophy of consciousness is exhausted.' He has reached this conviction after a remarkably just analysis of Kant, Hegel, Schiller, Nietzsche, the Frankfurt school, Husserl, Heidegger, Derrida, Bataille, and Foucault. I do not see how his account of the philosophy of consciousness can be much faulted.

The preposterous rarefaction is actually not the point. More important is the taking on board of the Eliot manner. The high judicial pose. The note of soliloquy rather than communication. Above all, the escape from personality behind an Olympian mask of critical detachment. What happens, though, when the man in the lecture hall next door, in off the fifties Dublin streets for his series of lectures, happens to be the poet Patrick Kavanagh?

> Every so often I have horrible moments when something keeps saying to me 'What right have you to be up there acting as one possessed by a God?' And unless I concentrate on the spiritual side I become ashamed and wish to run away and hide. Actually as week after week has gone by I have been more and more aware that any literary message I have had is not of the slightest consequence, that all I have to offer is myself. And bit by bit the clothing is being stripped from my personality.

Could any two passages be more innately antagonistic to each other? For Kavanagh, truth is personality, or 'the simple reality of a man' arrived at after a lifetime of complexes and affectations. For Donoghue, and for his selected masters Eliot, Yeats and Stevens, the high priests of artifice, truth is an escape from personality. It is as basic as that.

As for Eliot himself, with his hypernormal exterior, what was he escaping from? Night-wanderings in Boston, Paris and London at the start of the century suggest an abyssal cast of mind, as religiously drawn to Damnation as to Salvation. Lyndall Gordon, in her biographical studies of Eliot, presents these night-wanderings as the detached ironic observations of a poetical onlooker on the 'banality of vice'. That, I have to say, strikes me as the academic mind telling itself its usual politically corrected fairytales where sex, in particular, is concerned. Eliot knew the depths as well as the heights. His one contempt, a lifelong one it would seem, was for the liberalism of the middle ground, with its post-Enlightenment views, its illusion of moral progress and the calisthenic rigours of its 'healthy' sexuality. Anything, even Damnation in the Baudelairean sense, seemed preferable to that. On the other hand, with the dissipated nineties ghosts of Johnson, Dowson and Davidson looking over his shoulder, he knew perfectly well what Damnation meant, in real terms. The polite, impersonal man Donoghue describes meeting in the early sixties had real terrors to protect himself from.

> He was not cold, but evidently saw no reason for being warm in my favour. Still, I'm convinced that in his early years he had been a man of exceptionally intense and dangerous feelings. He feared for his sanity, and he had cause to fear for it. The demeanour he turned toward people was palpably a mask to conceal the feelings he lived in dread of. I see him as a character in a novel by Dostoevsky.

In all this, Wallace Stevens has not been forgotten. Eliot's great contemporary gets a walk-on part as a representative of that humanistic liberalism the Divine Vision has no time for. In a surprisingly unfair treatment, Stevens is presented only to be dismissed as an aberration out of the Enlightenment, a foolish believer in human self-sufficiency for whom 'all men are priests'. The poems chosen to illustrate this, and to set him, rather artificially, against Eliot, are far from his best and certainly far from his best known. The large-scale anguish of his finest work, which unites him with Eliot in the same essentially religious quest for order, Donoghue chooses to ignore. Instead, Stevens is presented as a kind of ladder to be kicked aside as Donoghue and Eliot step heavenwards together. One remembers that reverent reading of 'Sunday Morning' back in the UCD lecture theatre of the seventies and feels again the note of the disappointed infatuate. This time, however, infatuation has matured, not into love, but into a dry contempt for 'the senile humanist' who has 'the gifts reserved for age' still coming to him.

> Let me disclose the gifts reserved for age
> To set a crown upon your lifetime's effort.

First, the cold friction of expiring sense
Without enchantment, offering no promise
But bitter tastelessness of shadow fruit
As body and soul begin to fall asunder.
Second, the conscious impotence of rage
At human folly, and the laceration
Of laughter at what ceases to amuse.
And last, the rending pain of re-enactment
Of all that you have done, and been; the shame
Of motives late revealed, and the awareness
Of things ill done and done to others' harm
Which once you took for exercise of virtue.

The 'senile humanist', insofar as he is senile, will of course feel nothing of all this. In any case, he is Donoghue's, not Eliot's, creation. Eliot, perhaps because he had more to lose than most people by growing old and holy and universally eminent, is less inclined to religious self-satisfaction. The night-wanderings of earlier years are gone now – but so too is poetry, vitality. 'Words alone', in their closed autonomous realms of emotional depth, are a thing of the past. 'The poetry does not matter.'

If it doesn't, then the last three chapters, which deal with the *Four Quartets*, end with a rather odd contention. The *Quartets*, says Donoghue, are for people who only want poetry as poetry, not poetry as gratification of their sensual daydream or poetry as projection of their private lusts and vanities. In fact, it is not poetry that is at the centre of 'Four Quartets' but mystical experience, the intersection of time with the timeless, especially in the final one, 'Little Gidding'. This is usually spoken of as the *summa* of Eliot's later poetry, but it ends, for me at least, in the same rather wooden truce with the Furies that Ted Hughes speaks of in relation to the marriage that ends Shakespeare's last play, *The Tempest*:

And all shall be well and
All manner of thing shall be well
When the tongues of flame are in-folded
Into the crowned knot of fire
And the fire and the rose are one.

That is not poetry, at least in the 'words alone' sense of poetry, but the organiz-ing intellect, tying up the loose ends. A far wilder and truer ending to the whole sequence, and to the poetry as a whole, is the magnificent conclusion to the sec-ond quartet, 'East Coker':

We must be still and still moving
Into another intensity
For a further union, a deeper communion
Through the dark cold and the empty desolation,
The wave cry, the wind cry, the vast waters
Of the petrel and the porpoise. In my end is my beginning.

But Eliot, not being the later Yeats, did not go that open-ended road. On a lesser note, with Denis Donoghue himself, it is hard to say of *Words Alone* that its end is in its beginning. In fact, it ends very differently from the way it began. There is no circling back, no return to those insertions of the living person into the critique that characterized the early chapters. We end in the mid-air of impersonality, practical criticism. Infatuation, re-examined, has become love of a different kind, but Donoghue himself, the young man rushing at lunch-hour to grab the latest Eliot pamphlet at Hodges Figgis, has vanished along the way.

DENIS DONOGHUE, *Words Alone: The Poet T.S. Eliot*, New Haven & London: Yale University Press

Two poems

CONOR O'CALLAGHAN

Heartland

It's still going,
        the post-tea siesta
in the towns, and much later than planned,
        when I say my so longs
            and get away
into that antiquated heartland
        full of huckster shops
            and halls and the warmth
with which midsummer flatters itself.
        I make shapes,
            corkscrewing north
and fiddling now and then with the sunroof.

        After nine, ten,
            it's still good and bright.
So I pull over in Durrow
        for a pee, a cone,
            give the legs a bit
of a stretch and come around somehow
        to bluffing a bum
            with a plastered hand
about the Land Leagues and the famine
        in a hotel ballroom

where a two-piece band
is programming its drum machine.

Outside, on the green,
like from a shipwreck,
five Spaniards in a hired Toyota
have settled on
hitting West Cork
before the day's done. I run the motor,
flick on the lights.
What darkness follows
is just the Irish underwater darkness
of horse chestnuts,
handball alleys
and burger joints with hanging baskets.

The horizon
all the way up
goes into one of its purple patches.
On the roadside grazing
there are even sheep
marked with aquamarine, and midges,
and fields of rape
streaming towards
the dimmers. I pass out and am passed
by nothing. A tape
of bluegrass standards
meanders through both sides twice at least.

The shortened night

on the long finger,

between Monasterevin and Kildare,

for a minute,

or slightly more,

it starts to feel as if its shutter

won't fall again,

not properly,

or ever, and I am diving upwards

through seas of corn

or maybe barley

and any second now will break the surface.

Time-Zones

I drift on an ocean of eucalyptus.
An airbus, forty thousand feet up,
undoes the stratosphere's zip
and darkness opens out between us.

Sleeplessness. Homebirds in another room
are whimpering for me to call back across
an eight-hour lapse, the dawn chorus,
the landing I couldn't be further from.

We bring our long-distance silences to an end
(like Saint Brendan and Saint Patrick
arguing the toss mid-Atlantic)
still none the wiser where we stand.

By now you have long since tired
of the day I'm still midway through.
I can all but feel you ravelling the throw,
minutely, into your half of the world.

Through *Saturday Night and Sunday Morning*,
a late show, I blank out into the internal flight
that makes a straight line of the lights
of Baffin Island and the Black Mountains.

Standing here banging quarters into white space,
feeling like the next turn up on stage,
leaving message after disconsolate message,
sick of the sound of my own voice.

For the time being, being without yours
is being in love with this groundless
momentary displacement of hotel lounges,
a sweater folded around my shoulders.

Mostly, when sleep is beneath me,
I fall all over again for your absence,
the memory of your sap like absinthe's
aftertaste, your scent this near to me.

An afternoon in the eighties and it goes black
just like that, the way you envelop
yourself in your crushed velvet wrap.
I head back alone along the beaten track.

I guess I imagine you most while the elevator
is sighing through the motions back to earth
and I'm about to pass up, for what it's worth,
the lobby's foliage for the cold night air.

Time out with seconds to go for the Lakers
is suddenly a film of *The Tin Drum*.
In between, in fits and waves, the dream
of postcards arriving in my wake like echoes.

An hour to boarding, not expecting to, I get you.
The kids have gone down. You've just taken
your flip-flops into our west-facing garden
when the phone starts warbling out of the blue.

A biplane from the direction of Idaho
falls past the vanishing point across town
towards the very second it touches down,
a dragonfly landing on its own shadow.

For weeks there we come together
either side of the breakfast cereals:
you stepping out at Arrivals,
me still stuck in Departures.

Two stories

ELAINE GARVEY

Bedspins

Y. found me eating from the carpet and asked me why I was back on the floor again. I live on the floor, I said, it's where you should expect to find me.

I do, I live on the floor, close to the bed, the carpet under me. I need a bed leg to steady me; I could be on the floor or ceiling if it wasn't for the bed leg. From here I look out and see feet, they're enough. I lie on my belly when looking out, that way everything I see is touching the floor and I can tell how far away it is from the bed leg. Lying on my back is for music.

I eat whatever gathers on the carpet, which is not a state I'm proud of, but there's always something and it's a way of controlling the dust. There's plenty of dishwater as well, globules, grease, flat lather; it's all to go in. My taste is not distinctive, it all feels the same afterwards.

Being under the bed makes the floor seem closer, warmer. I'm a lateral thinker and I like the possibility to expand. And a cover. I can watch from the corners. I have to watch the dust, it loves under the bed maybe even more than I do, but it can have it afterwards, not yet. If I'm going to be there for a while I pluck at the black synthetic weave underneath to hear its song. I can read music, prefer music always. I do a little songing myself, high and quiet, but I've only one line: 'And then she left.' One line over and over. I never think of anything as blank because I know it's all filled with particles and joined by electricity, but when I'm songing I move to a place where all is joined by sound. It's floating along with free radicals, like water running through fingers.

As yet, I have only heard one voice, but I do see the faces in the black weave. The features are restless, moving about in new combinations all the time. The eyes usually move in pairs of different colours. It happened once that all the features flocked into groups, faces of ears and lips; the eyes were the best as I could not tell which way they were looking.

There are only two other places I would like to be: on grass with the bed over me, or in sand. Short fresh grass and a bed, but that could only be a holiday. Once the grass started to go yellow I'd have to go. The beauty of sand is there is no need for a bed, it's all particles and breathing. I will bury myself in sand.

I only found the floor after I met him. Maybe I would have found it anyway. He's a table boy, so he wanted me to sit close to him at the table with my chest above and knees below, but all of me would end up below. I slipped underneath so often our early days were spent by Y. coaxing me out. Y. says he knows about the faces and that I should not look at them because they will try to keep me when I should be leaving. They don't say anything, I tell him, they just move around.

He sat close to me today, gently tracing lines on my scalp. We don't say much, mostly vocables. He doesn't think I should be on the floor, I should go and stay with him. I asked about the bed there and he said its base goes right down to the floor. No bed leg. Couldn't even get my finger under it. What I need is not a bed leg, he says, it is to sit at the table close to him. Rather be close to the floor. I never know if he's going to shake me or not.

We met on the stairs. He was sitting with his fists under his chin and grabbed my leg as I passed, pulling me onto the step. I sat with him for a while and he moved his hand from my shoulder to my neck. I got used to his warm palm.

After he leaves I spend a long time under the bed. I open my spine in songing and move to a place of green and particles. I begin to doubt. It is hiding. I keep me here because it's quiet and close, no questions or answers demanded.

I get along with feet, we are both committed to the carpet. Toes are never intrusive. But hands. Thrusting into everything because they're closer to the eyes. They stick your eyeball on their fingernail and hold it up in front of everyone. You can't even cry about it.

All hands pulling at the bed to force me out. Why don't I leave the bed leg? They manage without one; but I see skirting, ladder rungs and banisters surrounding them. Y.'s hands are drum drumming on the table, waiting for me to come out. Maybe I should go. I *say* I want to. Sit at the table with my chest above and knees below.

This is how I get up. I place my palms on the black weave and push the bed on its side. The bed leg hangs between the floor and the ceiling. I stand, confronted by static faces, no more alone than before. I have never cried like this in the morning.

My back is cold, but I'm not songing to myself anymore. Louder, so much louder. I pick up fragments of limbs on my way down the stairs, torn ligaments and dislocated fingers. Outside I lay them in a circle because I like to pick over them at random and wince as I touch the nerve endings. Hands are not threatening when severed and removed from the eyes.

All day I look at cuts and bruises but I will do nothing to piece it back together, just morbidly fondle body parts. I recognize Y.'s fingernails on them, gently tracing lines between fine body hairs, kicking shins under the table. My own prints are there on the bruised flesh.

Once I break up the circle I bury the pieces in shallow graves and think of the bulging ground when I return under the bed. Eventually, Y. will not come back. Eventually, I will remember his fingernails more than his voice, which is what I plan for. After I bury myself I think of the congealing blood. Picking over my own circle. Safe as houses. Leg out of bed.

Body Armour

The foreman was the first to spot me watching from the bedroom. They're building a new railway; evenly spaced concrete sleepers, a double line for a better service. Although it's been over a month I haven't learned their names, but I wave all the same.

This is what I remember. I wanted to tell her. Leaning against the wall, my hair waiting for pigtails and stray light from the kitchen, or was it moonlight from the bathroom? I shouldn't dwell on this.

A hallway. From there. She came back, my mother, with a holdall, after midnight. I put on a jumper before going to meet her.

'Hello darling, did you miss me?'

Couldn't say it. Pulling threads from my belly. Her thumbnail had a raised centre, a ridged strip that she had grown. I asked her to fix my hair for school.

'Will you go back to bed then?'

'Yes.'

When we see that she isn't here in the morning, my older brother decides to light a fire. Underneath the choir in the old church is the best place for dead wood; Kevin says everywhere else has been looted for bonfires. He kicks out the last of the rotting uprights from the banister and we split as many pieces as we can against the steps. By the time we've carried our collection home, I have to tell Kevin I'm hungry and he makes peanut butter sandwiches for both of us. There are no firelighters, so I roll up newspaper and steal toilet roll cardboard for kindling. Kevin packs it into the grate, leaving out a corner for the match. He carries his own box now. The moss disappears before the flame, racing into smoke, and small insects change their hiding places. The wood doesn't catch.

> 'There was an old owl who lived in an oak
>
> The more he saw, the less he spoke

The less he spoke, the more he heard
Why can't we be like that wise old bird?'

Mrs Len gave me the book. You'll be fine, she said. She had a tricycle out the back that was missing all its tyres. I played here for the afternoon, driving the pedals as fast as I could until she sent me home at dinnertime.

Rolling out the scree today, giving turns to the onlooking children to go up the line. It's a uniform grey in the beginning, no diesel stains yet. One of them is banking up the dirt. Raised beds like a false avenue, that's how to spot them. The garden next door has a beech tree outside their fence, so they usually come and piss there. There's no embarrassment. What else can they do?

When no one comes in the night you must stop crying. This is the point where I stopped talking and started to forget, where the first tiny spots of the armour began to show. By the time she returned, it covered my body from the waist up.

I can hear the family in a green plastic tube behind the walls, driving through the joists. I heard them before, tunnelling into the windowsill. I drew miniature doors and mouse holes around the skirting boards in the bedroom, but they were rattling around the ceiling this time. From now on I leave the wardrobe door open, in case they make it through.

Perhaps it was the rain that woke me, or when she opened the bathroom door. I lay in the dark, listening, waiting to be certain. There was a new pressure around my throat, a constriction. I found her crouched in Kevin's doorway when I stepped into the hallway, her hand on the unopened bag. I sat with my back to the wall, facing her profile. The length of the silence depended on how far she had gone and I started to squeeze my toes, moving rhythmically from the outside in. This disturbed her, tugged at the corner of her eye. She turned to face me.

'Go on and get your hairbrush and I'll do it for you now.' Her hand was still gripping the side of the bag, but as she spoke the tension eased out from her fingers.

She knelt behind me to brush out the tangles. I could lie flat on my back or on my stomach when I went back to bed, but not on my sides. The bobbins would start to fall out if I did. When she finished, she kissed my crown and said I should get back under the covers.

That's it. My last memory. They're fastening the tracks with red curls today, little crooked smiles joining them to the sleepers. The uneven pieces have been cut and welded to fit.

Open letter to the Irish Tourist Board

ADRIAN FRAZIER

In October 2000 I was in Claremorris, Co. Mayo, for a weekend of events hosted by the George Moore Society. It was a Saturday afternoon. Earlier, there had been talks by Timothy Webb, Winterstroke Professor of Bristol University, the scholar-publisher Colin Smythe, and myself. Although the attendance was small, two dozen at its height, the speakers were not simply talking to one another; not quite. Some in the audience were descendants of Moore's tenants, some descendants of the Moores themselves, and one was a wild-eyed, craggy, eighty-year-old priest returned from Africa, who against instructions from his bishop had chosen to freelance in this particular parish. The crowd thinned away to almost nothing for the poetry reading by Patrick O'Brien and Rita Ann Higgins. They read to Timothy Webb, Colin Smythe, and myself. A few others arrived towards the end, including Tom Kilroy and Julia Carlson. After the reading the little gathering moved through the drizzling afternoon to Mulligan's next door, there to await the next event, the opening of an exhibition of landscapes by Brian Bourke.

In the pub, I learned that Tom Kilroy was an admirer of George Moore. We spoke of how strangely few of us there were at the George Moore Weekend. The night before, scores of young men and women had roared into Claremorris in new vehicles for the hotel disco (my hotel), and sang loudly up and down the footpaths at four o'clock in the morning, before ('Don't let him drive!' 'Get the keys off him!') driving off into the night; today the place seemed a ghost town. Opposite us, tacked up on the wall of Mulligan's, was the poster of 'Great Irish Writers'. Everyone has seen it: about sixteen photographs, all the same size, in black and white – Yeats, Shaw, O'Casey, Joyce, Swift, Kavanagh, Flann O'Brien, Synge, Lady Gregory, Beckett, Brendan Behan, and I cannot recall who else. But, as the playwright pointed out, you don't see George Moore on that poster. If that is a mistake, then one cannot just stick on another three-by-two-inch photo. Someone has to come off so that Moore can go on. 'Who would you take off?' I asked the playwright. Not missing a beat, he shot back: 'Behan.'

Now that strikes me as an excellent idea.

Brendan Behan's life (1923–64) is admittedly a ripping story. He was the son of an IRA man interned during the Civil War and the nephew of Peadar Kearney, author of the national anthem and many music-hall songs. He came from a long line of house-painters on his father's side, and thus is one of the few genuinely working-class Irish writers of distinction in the century. He was also arrested with an IRA gang for carrying explosives in Liverpool in 1939, and did three years as a Borstal boy. Shortly after his return to Ireland in 1941 he was sentenced to fourteen years in prison for shooting at a policeman; he was released as part of a general amnesty in 1946. He described himself as distressed as a result of being barred from communion on account of his IRA membership. He was precocious and self-educated. In *Dead as Doornails* (1976), Anthony Cronin writes touchingly of Behan spending days in the National Library reading accounts of Wilde's trials to find out just what queer things had been done with young boys, presumably so that he might do them too. Behan's autobiographical account of prison experience, begun when he was only eighteen, is his main prose achievement. His two successful plays also come of his experiences of crime-and-punishment – *The Quare Fellow*, a brilliantly unstructured and suspenseful dramatization of inmates at the time of an execution (literally 'gallows humour' about the Free State bureaucracy being simply the British state in different uniforms), and *The Hostage*, a slightly music-hall representation of an IRA kidnapping. After those plays, Behan provided public entertainment by getting drunk and cursing cheerfully on television chat shows. In a terrifying drive to drink himself to death, he cracked many jokes, terrific jokes, some of them. These gave life to a merry biography by Ulick O'Connor (1970), and also to a more recent and less merry biography by Michael O'Sullivan (1998). O'Sullivan tells us a good deal more than O'Connor about the appetites of Behan for his own sex (which don't fit with the Republican broth-of-a-boy Guinness poster-child image), and about the underbelly of an alcoholic's life: the times in hospital, the unfinished books, the rapid decay of his body, the beating of his very decent wife. The overall feeling one gets in contemplating the life of Behan is depression at the disastrous waste of talent because of drink.

Why is Brendan Behan loved? Well, he was both more alive and more funny than anyone, according to good judges who knew him before he was rotten with fame, people like Anthony Cronin and John Montague. He was a pub artist who talked away his best stuff, all lost in the ears of the crowd buying the drinks, except for those sayings recalled after his death or recorded in his sessions with the tape recorder. The wit and wisdom of Brendan Behan does not wear as well as that of Wilde, of course, but that is a standard no one surpasses. Behan had certainly mastered the syntactic principles of the epigram:

a) The definition: 'New York is my Lourdes, where I go for spiritual refreshment … a place where you're least likely to be bitten by a wild goat.' Or, better yet, 'A gentleman is a Protestant on a horse.'

b) The 'capping' comparison (as in 'To err is human, to forgive divine', or, as Updike amended it, 'To fuck is human, to blow divine'): 'To get enough to eat was regarded as an achievement. To get drunk was a victory.'

c) The rhythmically patterned sequence of clauses: 'I have a total irreverence for anything connected with society except that which makes the roads safer, the beer stronger, the food cheaper, and the old men and old women warmer in the winter and happier in the summer.'

d) The inversion of a commonplace (along the lines of Algernon's remark in The Importance of Being Earnest that 'Really, if the lower orders don't set us a good example, what on earth is the use of them? They seem, as a class, to have absolutely no sense of moral responsibility'): 'The conversation of the British upper classes is quite shocking to anyone who isn't used to it.'

e) The insulting analogy: 'Critics are like eunuchs in a harem – they are there every night, they see it done every night, they see how it should be done every night, but they can't do it themselves.'

Syntax aside, and the laughter over, the sense of these well-known quotations shows how Behan marketed himself as what British and American audiences wanted from an Irishman in 1960. Such jokes lampoon but also cater to the expectation that the Irishman will be a peasant from a still feudal Ireland. And sure, what could the starving man do when he got a few pounds but spend it, like a red Indian, on drink? In the social philosophy of Behan, mightn't there be a conflict between safer roads and stronger drink? And that 'old men and old women ... happier in the summer' is an utterly prostituted piece of sentimentality. One doubts that the young Behan – street smarts taken to the level of intellectual brilliance – would have given a fish's teat (to borrow a phrase) for the Brendan at the pitch of fame.

Yet that is the Behan who was immortalized. How did it come about? His ethos wasn't really in keeping with the practice (as opposed to the myths) of the Irish state in the first half of the century. Both Behan and his father were locked up by that state for political crimes. The early republicans were mostly Total Abstinence types, and believed along with a 1909 clerical correspondent to the *Leader* that the study of Irish prevented 'drunkenness, gambling, music halls, suggestive plays, and immoral literature' – prevented, in other words, Brendan Behan. The nationalists who minded the first decades of the Free State were not notably humorous, literary, foul-mouthed, heavy-drinking, or inclined to renew the physical-force campaign to end partition.

Was it that, in the midst of an otherwise wholly dead period of Irish theatre, Behan wrote two jolly and grim republican plays? In an essay from *Writing in the Irish Republic*, Chris Morash looks at Irish plays from the late forties and early fifties, and he notices in their stories of the twilight of the heroes, those who have to live through the reality of partition, when the patriots have become politicians, that there is a continuing sense of bitter belatedness, no great dreams left to be dreamed. In Walter Macken's *Home is the Hero* (1952), the father returning to his Galway council house from prison (there for manslaughter) finds that his wife is an alcoholic and his son wants to marry the daughter of the man he killed. There is no place at home for the hero. Such energies as those of the father in this play are the ones that came alive when the West was awake (1916–23). Honourable revolutionary violence has become just criminal violence. This is not a drama of inebriation, but of the subsequent hangover. Morash even thinks that Abbey director Ernest Blythe practiced a deliberate 'aesthetic of strategic boredom' in order to kill off hopes of a violent solution to partition. The kitchen set that had been an emblem of ur-Ireland had become no more than a kitchen again, and with little in the larder. Against this background, Behan's rebellious underclass jokes, his choruses of rebel songs, his quickness to throw a punch, his mad carnivalesque parody of true green republicanism, were both symptom of and salve to historical disappointments that followed the declaration of the twenty-six-county republic.

This diagnosis, however, is too local; his fame was global. His celebrity could not have happened without his explosive effrontery and lyricism, but Joan Littlewood and Jack Parr played their necessary parts. *The Hostage* was nearly as much Littlewood's *coup de théâtre* as Behan's play, new jokes being put in as the weeks passed or venues changed. On Jack Parr's *Tonight Show* in the USA, Behan was delightfully boastful and irreverent. He was soon called back for another visit, and by then he was known to over a hundred million viewers. For some, it was all to the good that he drank like a fish, cursed like a sailor, joined the IRA, went to gaol, wrote a bit in Irish, and did not work at writing books. Those are, by some lights, virtues. And I have some sympathy for them as virtues, to the degree that they at least achieve disreputability; they are anti-bourgeois, and delight in the customs of a clan as they may have been at one time, but are no longer.

For virtues and vices have a history and a geography too. They are not in one country what they are in another; and even within a single country, they change, sometimes rapidly. The era has passed in which lots of people would buy you a drink in New York because you had been imprisoned for IRA activities or thrown out of your hotel for making a scene. Yet public estimations of worth lag behind the underlying shifts of value. Behan's face remains on the poster, with a crooked grin.

While Behan is loved for his faults, George Moore is shunned for his virtues. From the time he was a young author, Moore fell under a cloud, and wherever he moved, the cloud moved too. It was a Victorian cloud, but it hung over Dublin as much as London, and it hasn't vanished yet. People are still somewhat ashamed of George Moore, whose guiding maxim in life was never to be ashamed. So what did Moore do wrong?

- He was a landlord.
- He liked Paris.
- He was a non-believer.
- He talked about sex frankly, and thought of it as an essential human delight.
- He thought contraception a moral obligation of humanity, because of over-population and the suffering of poor children.
- He thought nationalism a folly.
- He did not respect popular opinion.
- He laughed at democracy and socialism.

In short, he publicly insulted the idols of an earlier era: God, Chastity, Family, Patriotism, Public Opinion, and Democracy as the Infallible Guide to the Right Course of Action.

One might think that over a century after the Land War, it would not be held against Moore that he had been a landlord, especially in view of the fact (perhaps not widely known) that right towards the start of that conflict, in 1880 when he was twenty-eight years old and returning from Paris to Mayo, he saw the game was up for the feudal system in Ireland. He promptly decided to accept rent reductions, Home Rule, the sale of property, as they presented themselves to his consideration; they had history behind them. Three decades later, when his brother Maurice – a Gaelic Leaguer and nationalist himself – was still trying to hold on to a conception of a noble landlordism, GM made one last visit to Moore Hall to persuade him to sell the bulk of the estate. After a tender and beautiful recollection of the house as it had been, and a description of it as it was now in 1911, GM recounts in *Vale* a conversation with Maurice:

> We were kings in those days; little kings, but kings for all that, with power of life and death as has been said and truly, for we often sundered wife and husband, sister from brother; and often drove away a whole village to America if it pleased us to grow beef and mutton for the English market. And in those days the peasants were afraid to thatch their cottages lest their rent should be raised, nor was there one peasant in our villages or in the Tower Hill villages worth a ten-pound note. The Colonel asked me if I remembered a cabin in the middle of Annys bog, a dwelling hardly suited for an animal, yet a man and woman lived there and children were born in it, and I answered him: We used to pass it on our walks, you and I and our governess. Yes, I remember it, and I remember one day up in the mountains while grouse-shooting stabling my horse in a man's cabin. But we shall never be able to do it again. The landlords have had their day. We are a disappearing class, our lands are being confiscated, and our houses are decaying or being pulled down to build cottages for the folk. All that was has gone or is going. Moore Hall represents feudalism.
>
> I think [Maurice objected] that anybody would like to live in a comfortable house—
>
> Square rooms and lofty passages conformed to the ideals of our ascendants, and jerry-built villas, all gables, red tiles, and mock beams, stand

for modern taste and modern comfort; hot water on every landing and electric light. Nobody wants a real house unless an American millionaire, and it is not because of its reality that he wants it but for its unreality. It is unreal to him, and having a great deal of money, he indulges in eccentricity. In this way the old world is carried on by Americans; even in England there are very few houses that are the capitals of the estate they stand in as Moore Hall was up to fifty years ago. Moore Hall is out of date, and it astonishes me that you don't feel it. I wish in a way that I could summon sufficient courage to pull it down and sell it; it would make excellent rubble to build labourer's cottages, and if I could I would cut down every tree and lay the hillside bare. Why not, since I know it will be laid bare a few years after my death?

Pardon the length of this quotation, but one must furnish as testimony the author's own pulse of style in any claim upon the respect of posterity. Is he or she there present to us in the words, fully selved in the language, or is this simply a recombinant variant of forms of humanity already circulating in the sea of printed life? The future pardons least easily the affected, the proper, and the insincere.

This is a beautiful and Moorish passage, I think, because of the way reverie, direct discourse, free indirect discourse, and description arise and subside melodically. The elements of print-culture narration have been transformed to match both the movement of a mind and the needs of the storyteller's audience. The remarkable honesty of attitude is dependent on Moore's aesthetic of shamelessness. Because he has no impulse to apologize, he can fully recount the poignancy of an era of personal hegemony, one family over many, in both its charm (it was his only life, after all) and its evil (it was a life that bled other lives).

I read this passage from the steps of Moore Hall (burned out by the IRA toward the end of the Civil War) to a gathering of people who were interested in restoring the house as part of a rural development scheme. The Coillte-managed forests that surrounded us would be felled; the serpentine drive would be repaved, leading to a large parking area for tourist coaches. Boat rentals on Lough Carra, pony hire for children, the house restored for a George Moore summer school, a library, a Mayo genealogy museum and restaurant – you get the picture. After I read the passage from *Vale*, one man, a short man, bull-necked, broad-backed, with a cap, came up to me and said, 'He didn't have to pull the house down. We burned it out for him. Ha!' And now they wanted the government to rebuild it.

The Moore Hall Restoration Committee asked me to develop a use plan that met the objections of government to their current proposal (they said it needed a profit-making educational side). I sketched a plan involving an archive of all the Moores' papers, a local history and genealogy service, a rotating resident fellowship in Mayo literature and history or creative writing, a first-class restaurant, and seminar rooms, so that Moore Hall might be used as a conference centre for universities and others. Thinking of the ruined house, with thirty-foot trees growing up from the deep rubble of what had been its eighteenth-century roof, I had my doubts about whether it might ever make a twenty-first-century conference centre, and about what this might have to do with the writings of George Moore. Nonetheless, on 16 October 2000, along with a leader of the Moore Hall Restoration Committee, I met with Mr Eamon Ó Cuiv, then Minister of State for Arts, Heritage, the Gaeltacht and the Islands, in his Galway office. Would his department provide funding to match that of the County Council for the restoration of Moore Hall? His department could only look after properties that were in its possession, and Moore Hall belonged to the forestry board, or to the county, someone else, not to the government. Well, they could have it for nothing, he was told. But if they took it, Ó Cuiv replied, then they'd have to take care of it, and they had all too many old houses, once the homes of the gentry, to look after; everyone wanted to give them houses, and ones – mind you – that had not been burned out in 1923. Historic big houses! A few of architectural uniqueness they had accepted, but Moore Hall had never been architecturally unusual. There were lots like it. If people wanted a school or museum for the Anglo-Irish, in the name of their tradition, English writing of that class, that was very well, but they should go ask for funding from the Higher Education Authority or from the National University. They had lots of money. If it could be turned into a paying venture, for American students – he knew they were very interested in Anglo-Irish literature – perhaps it would work. The man from the restoration committee pointed out that they had been asked by his department to prepare a plan for the profitable operation of a restored Moore Hall, and now they had that. Would he care to look at the new proposal? No, why, if it was profitable, his department could not pay for it. They only maintained non-profit sites. The state could not meddle in the business sector. Thus the meeting ended, and the committee man made his sorry way back to Carnacun, County Mayo. And I, remaining in Galway, concluded that the fact that George Moore had been born into the landlord class was indeed still held against him ('their literature'), even though his manner of coming to terms with his birth order and class position seems pretty irreproachable.

If Moore's background hasn't helped his reputation, neither did his unbelief. Moore was the most frankly atheistical writer of importance during his era. He wrote about religion again and again, always from a materialist point of view: four novels about nuns – *Evelyn Innes* (1898), *Sister Teresa* (1901), *Heloise and Abelard* (1921) and *Madeleine de Lisle* (unpublished); a novel and a half dozen stories about priests – *The Lake* (1905) and *The Untilled Field* (1903); and one epic novel about the life of an unresurrected Jesus in a world without a personal God. It is not that he was a campaigning atheist; he was searching to understand how it was that some people could believe in such absurdity, and what it would be like to live under the apprehension that there was a God. Such stories are bracing and even painful for believers (as novels that are written by women from the male point of view are painful to men). Even unbelievers often feel that it is improper and perhaps immoral not to observe the social fiction that Christian doctrine is true.

Admittedly, Moore was sometimes liable to make deliberately offensive jokes on the subject. Once when he was in his seventies he visited along with W.K. Magee ('John Eglinton') St Winifred's Well in north Wales, where the sacred waters are believed to have the power to cure. It was here, reportedly, that in the seventh century St Beuno restored to his niece St Winifred both her head and her life after she had been decapitated by a rejected suitor. There was a turnstile at the entrance. When an old woman told Moore the price of admission, he was disgruntled. 'And how much for the cure?' 'At your age,' she replied, 'you ought to know it is by the grace of God!' Upon their departure (uncured), Magee – a Presbyterian preacher's son – asked Moore if he had no sense of the transcendent at all. Moore answered that there were many things in life he did not understand, and that he could admit there were other people whose understanding was greater than his own, but that, on the whole, life was 'no less wonderful for the materialist than for the transcendentalist – for Darwin, if you like, than for Kant'.

It was the next thing to a miracle, from GM's point of view, that humans arose from millions of years of animal evolution, and with splendid purpose in their eyes, built fanes of fruitless prayer, and rolled their psalms to wintry skies; it wasn't, as Tennyson thought, a picture of futility, but one of wonder that we had invented love, virtues, gods, and beauty not yet known in the world. We lived in awe of conceptions that arose from our evolution. It was astonishing that the most powerful human instincts – love, hunger, fear of death – could all be redirected, reshaped, even reduced to something else, by human belief. The moral utilitarianism of Christianity in its attitudes to love, appetite, and life itself – none to be enjoyed for their own sakes – horrified him. Whatever the case with animals, sex for humans seemed to him the source of so much more than offspring; it was the greatest heightener of the sense of life itself and the most profound passage of understanding between two people. It was a mystery to him why people should wish to overpopulate the planet and yet to avoid the pleasures of love. Moore was not without reverence, but he kept it for this life and our humanity.

While I believe that Moore has often been shunned for qualities that on reconsideration may actually be virtues, he does not get credit for conduct that is perfectly consistent with the moralities of everyday life, a table of virtues re-emerging in our own era.

- He believed in hard work.
- He did not drink to excess, ever.
- He told the truth (contrary to popular opinion).
- He did not spend lavishly, though he was liberal with hospitality and presents.
- He cared for the girl he believed to be his daughter.
- He allocated the Moore Hall rentals to his mother and brothers.
- He had a devout relation to the preciousness of his own individual being.

In *Confessions of a Young Man* (1888), the story of his mental divagations and dissipations, Moore says that even when he first came of age and into his fortune, his mother needn't have worried about him going to the dogs,

> ... for I was naturally endowed with a very clear sense of self-preservation; I neither betted nor drank, nor contracted debts, nor a secret marriage; from a worldly point of view, I was a model young man indeed; and when I returned home about four in the morning, I watched the pale moon setting, and, repeating some verses of Shelley, I thought how I should go to Paris when I was of age and study painting.

But I will not cite chapter-and-verse for all these aspects of his conduct; I wrote a very long biography that does that. I would say something of what makes them cohere and of what makes them relevant to us. One is the cardinal virtue, in the etymological sense of the word: the hinge upon which lesser attitudes turn. That is the last: he had a devout relation to the preciousness of his own being.

Moore acknowledged in *Confessions of a Young Man* a 'terrible and imperative … voice of the will to live', inherited 'from the elemental dust through countless generations'. He felt the capacity to create 'a complete and powerful self out of the partial self' which was all that the restraint of parents, schools, and churches had permitted him. And for that ghostly future self, he toiled like a slave; he watched over it; he cultivated it. Its invention was the toil of his years, drafts and revisions, and of those revisions more revisions. Drink would have warped his perceptions of his own instinctive nature. Truth-telling was both compulsory and desirable because only by sincerity could he become who he was. He did not spend lavishly to acquire things because value for him was in that which he could produce, not in what he could consume. To adapt Jesus's explosion of Judaic dietary laws, 'It is not what goes into a man's mouth that justifies him, but what comes out of it.' Of course, before we make a saint of Moore, it should be said that the Jesus of the Gospels did not urge people to reverence first of all the preciousness of their own being in this life.

If a resident alien can have an opinion on such matters, I think George Moore, slope-shouldered, self-mocking, is a possible hero for Ireland in the twenty-first century. It might be that if people knew about Moore, they'd like him; and if they thought more about Behan, they'd think twice about letting him keep his place on a poster-pantheon of literary heroes.

Most importantly, George Moore wrote better books than Behan did, by a long shot, though that would be irrelevant to the Irish Tourist Board as well as to American tourists. Yet I am too snobbish, and perhaps too cynical as well. Ethics may be irrelevant to canonization, and aesthetic distinction all that finally matters. Consider the case of Oscar Wilde. Scandalous conduct did not prevent his return to glory. In the 1890s he was gaoled, bankrupted, divorced, separated from his children, ostracized, and driven to live out his few last years on loans as a drink-sodden 'Mr Melmoth.' But the young kept returning to the sentences he wrote. How absolutely perfect! What a stylish way to be human! What a consolation that someone homosexual should be so superior and happy a human! Now he's Saint Oscar of The Wilde Century. It is always only a small number who give themselves up to the aesthetic life. There will also be in each generation some few who find in Moore's devious, disturbing, and lyrical narratives forms of the beautiful life, enhancements of being. They will draw off a little from the crowd, and meditate on their own condition; some will write, of him, of the world, or of themselves. Literature, real literature, imitates a rhythm or form, to which it imparts the distinction of personality, and this creates in some the desire to meditate upon that form, to celebrate and perpetuate it in other writings. That's a form of perpetuity with which Moore, and Wilde, and Behan too, would perhaps be gratified.

The Apocalypses

GEORGE SZIRTES

for Gerald Morgan

Death by Meteor

The night the meteor struck, the headline writers
were raising point sizes. The ten o'clock news
was brought forward an hour. In restaurants, waiters

ran from table to table. Theatre queues
were issued with free tickets. England was there
for the taking with Scotland and Wales. The pews

remained empty. Too late now for hot air.
This would be phlegmatic, immediate,
dignified, business as usual. Trafalgar Square

was full of pigeons. Trains would run extra late
until the shadow thickened sometime towards dawn
when the noise would be deafening. So they would wait

in streets or in pubs or on the well-kept lawn
of the bowling green, some tanked up with beer,
others with mugs of tea, some of them drawn

to familiar places, others steering clear
of all acquaintance. An Englishman's home
was the castle at the end of a frail pier,

the silence of a haunted aerodrome
where ghosts were running forward into fire.
Already they could hear the distant boom

of the approaching rock over Yorkshire,
the Midlands, Derby and Birmingham,
the pitch rising, ever sharper and higher.

Death by Power Cut

So one by one the fridge, the TV, the iron,
the radio, flickered, shuddered, and went out.
Nobody lit a candle. Not a siren

was heard, just cold and darkness and doubt
leaking away, becoming certainty,
like a hangover after a dizzying bout

of drinking, or a desire for terminal sobriety.
Out went the shop windows. Safeway's, Tesco's,
McDonald's, Boots, Woolworth's, the charity

stores, wine bars, offices, gyms, discos
and restaurants. It was the British winter
closing in for ever. Soon water froze

in the taps and the last of the cheery banter
died away. And the sea grew silent, the sky
fell like a pane of glass, one enormous splinter

of light, and broke across water. Not a cry
escaped their lips. They were proud in defeat.
They were a thirties movie and prepared to die

in black and white if need be, modest and discreet
as their fabled ancestors, thinking in
clipped tones. Then came a flurry of snow and sleet

that covered pavements up with dense white skin.
Lovers moved apart, as if afraid
Of what touch might do. The old would grin

And bear it. It was their finest hour. It weighed
on them like history. The darkness blossomed
in them. It was like moving into the shade.

Death by Deluge

I have seen roads come to a full stop in mid-
sentence as if their meaning had fallen off
the world. And this is what happened, what meaning did

that day in August. The North Sea had been rough
and rising and the bells of Dunwich rang
through all of Suffolk. One wipe of its cuff

down cliffs and in they went, leaving birds to hang
puzzled in the air, their nests gone. Enormous
tides ran from Southend to Cromer. They swung

north and south at once, as if with a clear purpose,
thrusting through Lincolnshire, and at a rush
drowning Sleaford, Newark, leaving no house

uncovered. Nothing remained of The Wash
but water. Peterborough, Ely, March, and Cambridge
were followed by Royston, Stevenage, the lush

grass of Shaw's Corner. Not a single ridge
remained. The Thames Valley filled to the brim
and London Clay swallowed Wapping and Greenwich.

Then west, roaring and boiling. A rapid skim
of Hampshire and Dorset, then the peninsula:
Paignton, Plymouth, Lyme, Land's End. A slim

line of high hills held out but all was water-colour,

the pure English medium, intended for sky, cloud,

and sea. Less earth than you could shift with a spatula.

Death by Suicide

It began with the young men. They lost touch
with something important almost as soon as words
entered their mouths. There was not very much

they could say with them. They ambled in herds
like sick cattle, bumping into the edges
of the world. People were sorry afterwards

though some were glad. They leapt off ledges,
drugged themselves, spun from light-cords, drew
knives across their necks. Their very bandages

were infected and their mothers knew
in odd dark moods that they were bound by fate
to join them. And so it spread, steadily through

the whole island, until it was too late.
Life had thinned to a fragile carapace,
bones turned to cartilage. There was a spate

of immolations in the Fens, a case
of hanging-fever in Derby, and a bus-load
of climbers cut their own ropes on the rock-face

at Malham. Whole families buckled. Death strode
through darkened living rooms where the radio
droned on, taking possession of one road

after another. Everywhere the sound of low
weeping. Some said it was mere melancholy –
you only had to listen to Elgar, the cello

concerto, to hear the national *folie*
de grandeur: all that aggression dressed
as modesty. Meanwhile the race was busily

killing itself, the sun was sinking in the west,
and one could read the experts' eyes, which were
distinctly bleary. They too were depressed.

The Three Remaining Horsemen of the Apocalypse

Then Fire, Famine, Plague, or what you will
(there was no energy left for War by then),
had drawn their horses up on a high hill

overlooking the city, to observe the men
and women below them. The air hung like ice.
The place had nothing to lose. They saw the pattern

of the everyday squeezed into one brilliant slice
of light. To them, each day sat somewhere
between desire and fear. Their paradise

comprised mere moments. A man in an armchair
was doing the crossword. A woman in a housecoat
was working at her window-box, her hair

gently fluttering across her exposed throat.
Two children were kicking a bottle. A dog ran down
an alley. The whole country seemed to float

like a vast web, unattached. They stood on the crown
of the hill and considered the course of history.
They watched as she progressed with a deep frown

along the river like Cleopatra, feeling sorry
for herself. I myself stared at the wall
of the yard trying to recall the memory

of other days like this. And then a miracle. Time stopped and was redeemed in the faint sunlight, the sun hazy, perfectly spherical.

The highest counter

TOM MAC INTYRE

Once upon a time there was a barber called Taylor, and, consequently, a tailor called Barber, a blacksmith called White, and, accordingly, a mute called Argue, a greengrocer called Pike, carpenter called Slater, undertaker Hope, tenor Crow, dentist Foot, beggar Cash, gelder called Love, butcher called Blessing, and thus, by decree, a watchmaker called Armstrong, Joe Armstrong, muscled and hirsute hoop of the strong arm, weal and woe of battle, clamour incessant, confronting the tiny wheels, filmy springs, and disappearing axles that were his *sotto voce* occupation and uncertain bread.

Enter – shop-window permanently shuttered – the dusk of Armstrong's premises. Admire, to your left, the tall counter, glass-topped, under the glass hundreds of watches, indistinctly labelled, condemned, asleep, forgotten – but brimming treasure-trove, witchery of dial, hands, silver, gold, blurred amalgams, you could devote all you possessed – or were possessed by – to their choiring stillness. Armstrong would have heard the door, would, when it suited, appear, lanky, bald, granny spectacles, merry grimace his unalterable greeting, and a single sentence – *Spuds and rain and the Carrick train* – from which he had, since the day of its inception, gleaned small but sufficient portions of contentment.

Right inner corner of the cramped customer zone, a stoically frenetic grandfather clock. Its eye – you could tell, subfusc or no – was on the high counter. As was yours. Measure that counter, mentally at least, every time you see it. Touch it every second time, let its manna nourish your initiate cells. It has claims to the fabulous, the mythic, nothing like it in these parts, it was from some previous patrician century or scarcely imaginable heroic age, boasted brass folderols and intricate panelling, invited and withheld, pacing shyly mature. Its central assertion of cachet was of a piece, had to do with its being stained by blood, blood which, in the event, had not been shed, and so had room to lave that counter in perpetuity, come and go, hypnotic and endearing.

An ordinary breakfast-time in the frowzy Armstrong kitchen. 'It's the salt makes the stirabout,' Joe had commented – ritual contribution – as he finished the first course. 'As stirabout the salt,' Sadie, the wife, advanced her melodic and biblical reply. The boiled egg followed – for Joe. Sadie did not eat eggs, and, a natural progression, was plagued by neighbours bringing gift-eggs, hen-eggs, goose-eggs, duck, bantam, and once, Seán Sands, the stone-mason, brought seagull-eggs from a summer watering-hole much in vogue. (Sadie disposed of surplus eggs by flinging them into the fields on her rare evening walks.) But breakfast. Joe, boiled egg consumed, is, for recreation, flaking the shell, a warm brown, deftly freckled, dropping the fragments on to the oilcloth – pallid cherry-blossom against off-white – which protected the long-suffering deal. Sadie asked him to desist. He obliged, resumed the exercise. Sadie left the table.

Hours pass, not many. We know what Sadie was about in her bedroom – or know in broad terms, she was remarked cleaning a window. Equipped only with rag and spittle – a detail which gained general approval – she washed and polished the window over and over, bringing those wilting panes to an unparalled sparkling brilliance. Then, applying the same dedication, same rag and pliant spittle, she brought them back to their habitual dingy condition. Astute spectators – there were two, brother and sister, pensioners, next door – were entranced by the drama of Sadie's steady coming to visibility in the window, contrary reduction to fog and mist, the bold connection between those paired movements and her life to come – this day, and across years in store.

Two o'clock, and Armstrong is behind the counter, turning the labelled watches in their sleep, petting his magnifying glass. In the kitchen, dishes washed, Sadie puts on an apron, polka-dotted navy blue, never before worn, selects her weapon, standard carving-knife, secretes it in her right wellington – she never wore shoes – and makes quietly for the shop. Sadie: soft-footed, reclusive, morose within limits, her people of the type 'inclined to cry when night comes'. She reaches the shop, short corridor from the kitchen plausive behind her. Joe, looking up, is struck by the calm in her demeanour. 'What were you at?' he asked, not unfriendly. 'Cleaning a window.' 'Good woman yourself.' 'Then I dirtied it again.' 'Always the conservative.' 'Not always,' Sadie demurred. Joe didn't pursue it. Sadie stood there. 'Seán Sands might be glad of those goose-eggs the Lynch woman brought,' he threw out. 'Never,' Sadie said, 'They're for the fields.' No harsh note, everything nice and handy. 'Farmers won't thank you for upsetting the cows,' Joe conjured lightly, went on to prod, 'Didn't they blame you for a shore taste in the milk from those seagull-eggs?' 'Cows don't eat them eggs,' Sadie spoke evenly, 'They just lick them, let them lie.' Joe enjoying this pastoral cameo, Sadie reached into the wellington, still about her that inex-pressible calm, limpid chasuble of her own inspired design. 'What went through your mind when you saw the knife?' Joe was asked by the many. 'What did you see – besides her level features – in that moment?' 'Flakes of the breakfast egg,' he'd reply. 'Wet-day funeral, not much fuss or bother. Sadie by the grave – special permission, that face on her, exact same.' He confessed to some that he was overwhelmed – at the time, and retrospectively – by 'the justice of her cause'. Not immobilized. As Sadie moved to deal with him behind the counter – she must have seen him as trapped within – Joe stood up, weighed her. She was beside him. Blade descending, he vaulted – jumped – flew – the counter, departed the shop, secured aid. Sadie made no resistance, smiled as she was taken away.

And in the twenty years of her stay in The Big House – where she died peace-fully – was a model inmate. She had little to say but she said it often, and so it passed into legend. On the day of her arrival, and ceaselessly thereafter, she stated her one regret – she had never been to New Zealand. Some antipodal lunge in that *New Zealand* – and a primal conviction in the voice – ensured her a captive and enduring audience. As a young woman, she recited, the chance was hers, return ticket, all arrangements – courtesy of Aunty Eileen – comfortably in place for a three-month stay, but something had gone wrong, a death, an illness, some family dispute, and the plan dissolved. Now she'd never go. As she'd suspected – indeed known – at the time. 'It's the most beautiful country,' she'd conclude. 'In this world.'

Edna Longley's map

PETER SIRR

Where does poetry criticism occur today? Who are its producers and consumers and what is their relationship with each other? In Ireland poetry criticism occurs, as far as the non-specialist is concerned, in the form of brief summary-reviews in one or two newspapers. These are rarely more than thumbnail sketches, tiny critical cartoons indulged by literary editors as a kind of half piety towards a form that was once thought important but has long since been super-seded, in terms of space and prestige, by prose fiction, biography, history, politics, or, for that matter, cookery, gardening, feng shui. For the semi-specialist there are the 'trade journals', which publish longer reviews and articles. These are mostly written by poets and vary widely in quality and intent. And then there are what Louis MacNeice called the big critics, people who write whole books, as opposed to the little ones who grind out the cartoon reviews. These days the writers and the consumers of whole books of criticism tend to be aca-demics. This has several effects. One is that a good deal of poetic discourse happens in the absence of poets, or at least of those poets who are not also crit-ics. The other is a tendency of practising poets to eschew criticism altogether, or to confine themselves to the occasional review or statement. They are more likely to give interviews, and thus the interview has become a kind of etiolated critical form. And there is an ever-growing chasm between the theory-driven crit-ical concerns of university-based critics and the critical prose produced by poets.

All of this is, I think, ultimately impoverishing for poetry, because poetry cannot take place in a vacuum; the success of any artform is at least partly wed-ded to the quality of its reception. A culture that ignores poetry can drive poets into an isolated cadre in which practitioner speaks to practitioner or initiated adept. Equally damaging can be the culture that blandly accepts everything with the open arms of cheerful indifference. In Ireland today the critical thinness coincides with the rhetoric of democratization, which turns everyone into a potential producer and is not really interested in what happens to the product.

Another effect of the critical silence of many poets is the absence of real engagement with the work of others. In one of the essays from her new collection, *Poetry & Posterity*, Edna Longley quotes Donald Hall:

> Most poets need the conversation of other poets. They do not need mentors; they need friends, critics, people to argue with … The history of poetry is a history of friendships and rivalries, not only with the dead great ones but with the living young.

This has the sound of a long-gone age. I take Hall's 'conversation' to mean a serious critical engagement, and, among poets in Ireland, this is a scarce enough commodity. Maybe it is because we have entered a phase of our culture that prefers publicity to criticism, advertising to the adversarial, where opposition is taken as a sign of that long-banished vice, begrudgery, and the chief function of the critic is to endorse, or ignore. It could also be argued that soft criticism produces or encourages soft writing; criticism that doesn't distinguish between the trite and the accomplished ends up narrowing the spectrum that poetry occupies.

There was a time when things were different. In her essay on Louis MacNeice as critic, Longley quotes an article on F.R. Leavis by Stefan Collini which remembers that in the middle decades of the last century the place where the big questions were asked, where 'debates [took] place in which a society's conception of itself [was] fought out and fought over, in which standards of argument, of intellectual and aesthetic excellence, even of general human flourishing, [were] articulated', was literary journalism. That the canvas of criticism, particularly where poetry is concerned, has shrunk steadily over the years is a recurring concern of Longley's book. In 'Irish Bards and American Audiences'

Longley quotes Dana Gioia's comment in 1992 that 'the traditional machinery of transmission – the reliable reviewing, honest criticism, and selective anthologies – has broken down'. What has replaced the traditional machinery, according to Gioia, is a culture of mutual congratulation and blurbspeak. Even allowing for the fogeyism that licenses each generation to feel that it occupies the lowest pit of poetical/critical despond, things have genuinely disimproved since MacNeice was writing, both because the outlets that sustained writers like him – the non-academic, non-specialist publications – have mostly ceased to exist, and because of the institutional proliferation of poetry. The professionalization of poetry within American universities has fostered a self-serving timidity masked as generosity of spirit; Gioia got that right, and the situation is no better today. The circumstances in Britain and Ireland are very different, though the results are much the same.

Longley's diagnosis of the ill effects of the 'pseudo-democracy spreading along the literary trade routes to Britain and Ireland' is only a small part of the argument in this essay. She begins with a parable: the arrival in Dublin in 1996 of the US aircraft-carrier *John F. Kennedy* and the adulation with which it was met (though she concedes that 'a few hundred people protested on the quay'). Many others in fact protested in print, but it is true to say that in terms of the media and the general public the visit was enthusiastically embraced (though Longley's comment that 'The women of Dún Laoghaire made up for missing the Second World War' is surely unnecessary). The parable continues: 'Several days later two British naval mine-sweepers paid a goodwill visit to Cork. A Sinn Féin councillor objected.' The apparent point of this parable is to demonstrate Ireland's embrace of US colonialism while remaining highly sensitive to 'the merest sighting of British forces'. How a single Sinn Féin protest, against the hundreds she has already, somewhat reluctantly, conceded attended the *JFK* arrival, is supposed to illustrate this is anyone's guess, but it does reinforce the feeling that Longley is unable to resist any opportunity to sneer at the Republic. The real point of this piece is to show that 'In the US a corporate merger between Celticism and Irish-

American Catholic sentiment ... removes guilt as it disguises power.' American academics studying Irish literature 'ipso facto revoke their complicity in anything "Anglo". It's like being able to watch *Braveheart* with a clear conscience.'

Whatever about differences of emphasis and political perspective, it's certainly true that the tendency for Irish writing to be swallowed by Irish Studies and fed into a narrative of Irishness and Irish history effectively imprisons it. It also excludes any variety of Irish writing that doesn't accommodate this narrative, doesn't foreground Ireland itself – and preferably a version of rural Irish experience. Edna Longley may profess impatience with the discourses of Irish Studies, but they are her meat and drink. And a sad irony of the relentless dominance of concerns with identity is that writers who can't be written about with reference to one 'identity-discourse' or another are left out in the cold both by Longley herself and by the Irish and American critics she joins battle with. Many Irish writers, it should be said, haven't been shy of promoting their Irishness in the US, even (consciously or unconsciously) allowing a marketable version of Irishness to take up the central position in their aesthetic. Few Irish critics comment on this, which makes Longley's sharp deconstruction of the Irish Studies industry welcome. She takes the reception of Eavan Boland's work as symptomatic of the problem. In Boland, versions of Irishness and feminism combine to produce a vision few feel able to criticize, and Longley notes the tendency of critics to take the poet on her own terms, blandly accepting her own statements about her work. In a culture where poets smilingly attend papers on their own work (as Longley claims to have witnessed) and where the mission of the dismal *Irish Literary Supplement* is to celebrate and promote, a cosy interdependence develops between the approved poets and their celebrants. Those unlucky enough (or lucky enough) not to be invited to the feast will be doomed to relative invisibility as long as the critical framework is determined by the large corporation known as Irish Studies.

Longley's book is explicitly concerned with audience, that of the future as well as the present. One of the conclusions posterity will surely arrive at is that

Irish literary discourse was the most inward-looking on the planet. Debate in Ireland inevitably means debate within the parameters of Irishness, and any outward reference, any engagement with the world of not-Ireland, must be fed back into the maw of our self-concern. We are a very long way still from the time devoutly wished for by Derek Mahon when the question of who was or wasn't an Irish poet would clear a room in seconds.

There are of course endless reasons for this preoccupation. The isle is full of the noises of competing 'identity-discourses'; nationality and literature feed directly off each other in a way they do not in other cultures, and criticism tends to be an extension of politics by other means. What might be surprising to an outsider is the relentlessness of these connections and the inexorability with which succeeding generations of Irish writers and critics reach for them. It's a small country, and the vigour with which we gaze at ourselves has to do with that smallness; our claims of distinctness have for so long rested on fictive visions of ourselves that we don't feel we can command anyone's attention – not even our own – without them.

The central essays in *Poetry & Posterity*, contrary to the blurb's claim that the book 'marks a move back from Irish culture and politics to poetry itself', are intensely preoccupied with the politics of identity, with competing narratives of history, competing critical ideologies. 'Northern Irish Poetry and the End of History' situates itself very clearly in its historical moment, beginning with a precise list of the incidents that took place after its title was conceived: 'the Canary Wharf bombing (February 1996); the Manchester bombing (June 1996); the murder of Garda Gerry McCabe in Co. Limerick – by the IRA (June 1996); the murder of a Catholic student and taxi-driver, Michael McGoldrick – by Loyalists (July 1996); the murder of Lance-Bombardier Stephen Restorick – by the IRA (February 1997); the murder of a Catholic, John Slane – by Loyalists (March 1997) …' The title refers to the end points sought by both traditions and to the degree to which Northern Irish poetry is bound up with 'Irish history'. The essay, which is as much a study of Irish historiography as of poetry, proposes that Northern Irish poets 'have shared a raised consciousness of history' and that this 'has tightened the intertextuality between poems, and between poetry and other written and unwritten texts'. Poets, in other words, like historians, speech-writers, newspaper editors or graffiti artists, are highly aware of each other and define themselves in relation to the endlessly self-perpetuating historical space they occupy. Longley is at least as interested here in the ideological 'inventions' of Ireland by critics and historians as in the work of poets. Her bottom line is that Irish literary and cultural criticism has conformed to a post-colonial, nationalist reading of history – one of the constantly recurring themes of the book – and is not interested in imagining any other terms:

> To summarise the dialectics between these stories of Ireland: for Garvin as for Kiberd, 'Irish history' in the old sense has ended: there is an achieved 'pattern', 'completion' – and Garvin explicitly inserts the Northern Irish 'peace process' into his reconciliatory conclusion; for Smyth as for Deane ... there has been neither end nor birth but a continuing circle or unfertile set of oppositions.

In Northern Ireland, the end of history is the cessation of years of violent conflict but also the point envisioned by both traditions – British withdrawal, the end of the Union – as either goal or apocalyptic terminus. Longley cites the unionist political scientist Arthur Aughey, who 'points out that unionists distrust all language of movement and "process" because they read it as propelling them in one direction only – towards a United Ireland'. The literary imagination that responds to this situation tends to alternate between 'apocalypse and utopian nativity'. It's not easy to see what the role of poetry is for Longley in this situation. She looks at the different responses of some poets to recent events including the ceasefire: the relative optimism of Heaney's 'Tollund' (faulted for 'a slippage into nationalist vocabulary' in its last line); the ambivalent gesture of Michael Longley's 'Ceasefire'; an upbeat 'blueprint for redemption' in Mahon's

'The Hudson Letter'; Ciaran Carson's comic relish for narrative; Muldoon's irony. She looks to them as 'poet-historians' and expects of them a form of enquiry and even of resolution. She expects her poets to inhabit the historical moment and to find their truest definition there. 'Some people read Irish history as poetry. I prefer to read poetry as history.' The implication here is that poets are more trustworthy interpreters of history than historians, literary critics or cultural commentators, precisely because poetry is less conclusive, less absolutist, cagier in its deployments, less subject (with certain slippages) to ideology. Poetry is a better sort of politics.

It's not a reasoning everyone will accept, and it assumes a role for poetry that many would resist. For Longley, though not for everyone, 'Mysteriously, how history judges poetry depends on how poetry judges history.' Not that there's anything new about this conclusion, which is essentially a re-statement of the position articulated in an earlier essay, 'Poetry and Politics in Northern Ireland', reprinted in *Poetry in the Wars*. There, she quotes Louis MacNeice's preface to his *Modern Poetry* – 'The writer today should be not so much the mouthpiece of a community (for then he will only tell it what it knows already) as its conscience' – and finds the Heaney of *North* guilty of alignment with 'one Ulster community'. Protestant poets, on the other hand, 'have no trouble getting their critical faculties going'. She is relieved to turn from the surfeit of history in Seamus Deane and Tom Paulin to Mahon's figure 'through with history' or Paul Muldoon's subversive metamorphoses. That essay concludes by suggesting that poetry's true path is neither 'atavistic boreen nor humanistic motorway' but resides in the freedom of intelligence and scrupulous neutrality.

Some neutralities are more neutral than others. Part of Longley's neutrality is to root out and expose all traces of Catholic/nationalist/Celtic mythology. 'The Poetics of Celt and Saxon' looks at the endurance of the Arnoldian stereotypes of poetic Celt and prosaic Saxon. Recent celebrations of Irish culture – in Germany and France – have generated an image of Ireland as an otherworldly poetic domain unrecognizable to the Irish participants. Ireland may be partially complicit in these stereotypes, but no one should underestimate the enduring strength of the prejudices embedded in one culture's perception of another: the French and Germans need no help from Arnold or Bord Fáilte in their loyalty to a romanticized 'Celtic' vision. But of course it is also true that we continue to sell Celticism to ourselves in the form of products appeasing spiritual hunger, and Longley is surgical in her tracing of a book like John O'Donoghue's *Anam Cara* back to Arnold, Renan and Ossian.

It is also true that this is only one part of a complex story and that it is increasingly difficult to represent reality in the Republic in terms of a single narrative. Although Longley is grateful that nationalist ideology is in decline, banished to the sidelines by the diminished authority of the Catholic Church, the materialism of the new economy and distrust of 'northern absolutisms', she is bothered by what she sees as a cultural neo-nationalism. In terms of poetry this means that 'Celticist notions cling to poetry in ways that can be either positive or problematic'. She goes on to argue that Irish nationalism has not been slow to exploit Celticism to its own advantage and that poetic relations between England and Ireland are muddled by 'the hidden workings of ethnocentrism'. She feels, for example, that Declan Kiberd is more in thrall to Celticism than Yeats ever was. And Seamus Deane, though ostensibly critical of the romanticizing of the Celt, slips irresistibly into 'Celtic-poetic recognition factors' in his autobiographical novel *Reading in the Dark*. 'It is an irony (which Yeats might enjoy) that Deane's mildly Celticist fiction should reach a wider audience than his anti-Celticist criticism.' Longley considers Heaney's treatment of Englishness in the famous essay on Hughes, Larkin and Hill, 'Englands of the Mind', arguing that Heaney as an Irish 'Celtic' poet overvalues the Anglo-Saxon qualities perceived in Hughes and Hill. Anglo-Saxonism, with its emphasis on origins and a remote past, is only a short hop from Celticism. *Beowulf* is too close to the Bogside for comfort. In Heaney's criticism 'Anglo-Saxon has become the new Gaelic'. Larkin is less authentic than Hughes and Hill because his England is less connected to its roots. Heaney 'restores to England, via Northern Ireland, nineteenth-century ethnocritical concepts'. Some of this is fair comment, as is her criticism of Heaney's mythologizing of the differences, often in gender stereotypes, between the Irish and English languages, Celt and Saxon, Planter and Gael, in the poems of *Wintering Out* and *North*. And she applies similar strictures to Tom Paulin, whom she sees as having fallen 'for the idea that language and racial/cultural character are intimately connected'.

All of this just goes to prove that criticism in Ireland is trapped within a self-perpetuating cycle of obsession and seems doomed to proceed for some time yet as a set of binary oppositions. It's easy to sympathize with Longley's criticism of an ethno-centred discourse, easy to see why she can be irritated by figures as diverse as Hughes, Paulin, or Heaney at his most 'Celtic'. But Longley's answer is hardly thrilling. Faced with the perceived ethnocentricity of Celtic/Catholic/post-Catholic/nationalist poets and critics, she retreats into a grim parochialism, a Northern Ireland of the mind characterized as much by what it excludes as what it chooses to shine its torch on. There are, probably, hearts that warm to titles like 'American Influences on Northern Irish Poetry in the 1960s', but one could wish for wider horizons. When they do extend beyond Northern Ireland her horizons tend to be defined by the lyric tradition exemplified by Thomas Hardy, Edward Thomas, Philip Larkin and early Auden. There is of course a natural continuity that links these poets with MacNeice, Mahon, Hewitt and Michael Longley, and she is a perceptive analyst of that tradition. Her devotion to that tradition, and to the meshing of poetry and politics in Northern Ireland, seems to preclude an interest in other poetries: American, Australian, English-language poetry outside the particular tradition she has made her specialty, even poetry from south of the border.

The poets that are on her map, like Edward Thomas, MacNeice and Larkin, are poets who work within an English tradition, extending it rather than reinventing it: they are insiders who subvert from within, who are not always what they seem, whose work has a social resonance, a strong sense of its own audience. A long essay on Larkin is a deliberately psychological reading of this poet of the 'mask-lyric', whose iconic status as a poet of England and Englishness concealed the loner who cultivated an aestheticism modelled on Yeats. She reads him as a *fin de siècle* decadent given to fetishizing women. Larkin's work keeps women at a distance, to be idealized or dismissed. Longley analyzes Larkin's psychology – using evidence from his letters and from Andrew Motion's biography as well as from the poems – because she wants to know 'why aestheticism attracts a certain kind of psychology, and how this influences Larkin's lyric'. She spends considerable time arguing that Larkin was a narcissist whose conception of his art was grounded in his withdrawal from the world. 'His poems and letters reiterate the fear of being invaded, diluted, controlled or possessed by another. Spending the self is equated with spending money – you don't get it back.' She suggests, I suppose successfully, that 'borderline narcissism fits the conflicts that Larkin's poetry both manifests and explores', demonstrating instances of Oedipal conflict, narcissistic rage, inwardly directed desire. 'There may be parallels here with Woody Allen. Larkin and Allen share eccentric looks, defensive wit, incapacity to cohabit, obsession with death ... agoraphobia, phobia about daily minutiae, an interest in youngish women, self-fascinated self-analysis.' Larkin is, in other words, a thoroughgoing neurotic, his poetry a continual psychic crisis-management. Why does this matter? Larkin never wrote a well-adjusted poetry, but there is a comedy in the gap between the public perception of Larkin and the bilious neurotic who emerged in the *Letters*. 'One factor in the shock caused by Larkin's letters was a feeling that he had been taken to the bosom of England under false pretences – a serpent indeed.'

All of this seems to go to show 'that lyric poetry originates in the cry of primary narcissism against ultimate doom'. The essay is good on Larkin's solitariness, his aesthetic of the solitary trying to connect with a version of the social world. This is where Longley excels; her real talent is connecting poetry with its socio-historical context. This is hard on poetry that operates at a remove from its contemporary moment, but it makes Longley a formidable reader of her chosen writers, alert to Edward Thomas's 'eco-radicalism', or to Patrick

Kavanagh 'taking the strain of his journey from small farm and self-contained Catholic community, from claustrophobia to agoraphobia, see-saw[ing] across several historical faultlines'.

To read *Poetry & Posterity* is to feel that Longley's core vision of poetry has altered little over the years. She remains wedded to the idea of poetry as a superior form of rational discourse. She occasionally looks over the fence to giggle at the cluttered gardens of the neighbours. 'Who would want to go to bed with a Language poem? A masochist, possibly.' Yet a lifetime in bed with Edward Thomas or Louis MacNeice might also begin to pall. She has a very definite sense of poetry as a singular entity and is impatient with pluralisms like 'poetries'. There is the sense of choices long made; to call a book *Poetry & Posterity* is, after all, to stake a very definite kind of claim, and the act of editing an anthology, which she has also recently done, a further extension of that claim. Her essay on British anthologies of the twentieth century is hard on those that try to be inclusive and shy away from judgement, or that allow themselves to be subject-driven; she is equally hard on anthologies that push different 'lines' of poetry, that have separatist agendas which in her view simplify tradition. She is particularly annoyed at anthologists – Andrew Crozier and Tim Longville in *A Various Art*, Michael Schmidt in the *Harvill Book of Twentieth-Century Poetry in English* – who take their cue from American poetry, or view modernism as an American affair with a British satellite, or 'subscribe to different types of collusive Anglo-American narrative'.

If, in her impatience with ideologically driven versions of poetry, Longley were advocating an openness that allows very different kinds of poetry to co-exist and speak to each other, then her impatience would be welcome. But she doesn't really step outside the circle of her own chosen poets to direct a curious glance at a different kind of poet. Her battle with modernism, articulated again in the preface to her anthology, *The Bloodaxe Book of 20th Century Poetry*, is a battle against those who use it to proscribe traditional forms or traditional ideas of coherence, who take the view that the appropriate response of poets is to mimic the instability and fragmentation of the world and of language, or who misread supposedly 'traditional' poets and fail to recognize that modernity is a many-coloured thing. Longley is right to defend poetry against all 'isms', but I can't help feeling she becomes too embattled in her defence of a particular lyric norm, and as a result closes herself off to poems that aren't articulated from a central, authoritative self.

Her own anthology comes freighted with its share of arguments and is quite clear about the version it offers of twentieth-century poetry from Britain and Ireland. The first, important choice it makes is to be highly selective: there are fifty-nine poets here, represented by between three and eleven poems. In her essay on anthology-making Longley criticizes some of the recent anthologies for offering too many poets, citing, for instance, the *Penguin Book of Poetry from Britain and Ireland since 1945*, edited by Simon Armitage and Robert Crawford, with its 141 poets, 55 of whom are represented by a single poem, or Seán O'Brien's *The Firebox*, 62 of whose 126 contributors are represented by a single poem. This is a real dilemma, and it's one shared by many poetry magazines. Generosity and inclusiveness are the virtues proclaimed. But what poet can be judged by a single poem? Longley responds with Hardy (11), Yeats (10), Edward Thomas (11), D.H. Lawrence (8) and on with Sassoon, Muir, Eliot, Gurney, Rosenberg, MacDiarmid, Owen, Graves, Stevie Smith, Kavanagh, MacNeice, Auden. Recent poetry is represented by Heaney, Mahon, Longley, Muldoon, Carson and younger poets like Armitage, Paterson, Jamie and Duhig. The space afforded to each will make this a genuinely useful book for many, an ideal teaching anthology, and each poet is usefully introduced at the beginning of the selection. Being generously selective or selectively generous entails making decisions, and Longley is not shy of stating the larger ambition of this anthology, which is to present 'the most significant poets of our time'.

Clearly, Longley's version of the most significant poets will not be shared by everyone. And despite her strictures about 'subject-driven' anthologies – 'You will not get lost here as in other anthologies – with their vast lists of poets sum-

moned up to serve a critic's argument or to illustrate a journalistic overview',
the blurb assures us — her own collection is the fruit of a considered argument.
The first part of that argument – leaving aside the question of who is chosen,
whose work is considered 'key'– is to focus on a certain kind of poem: 'This
anthology is essentially an anthology of 20th century lyrics.' Part of this comes
from her feeling that the restitution of the concentrated, fully articulated lyric
is one of the century's core achievements. She cites for instance Yeats in his preface to his notorious Oxford anthology relishing the freedom of preferring 'the
acorn to the oak'. Part of Longley's point is that we're likely to forget the extent
to which poetic ambition tended in the nineteenth century towards the long
poem, and that the modernist project in its turn has tended to devalue the lyric
in favour of the big, flailing, fragmented epic of 'The Waste Land', 'Briggflatts',
the Cantos or 'Paterson'. The first two are represented by extracts, but apart
from them the book is dominated by what used to be called the 'well-made
poem'. The only problem with Longley's approach, though she wouldn't see it
as a problem, is that it necessarily excludes a great many poets whose work is as
'key' as any here but doesn't adhere to the vision of lyric that she cherishes.
There's little here that's experimental or formally risky. Longley is entitled to
her aesthetic choices, yet she sometimes seems happy to discount alternative
poetic values altogether rather than allow that other choices could have been
made. Thus she can blithely inform us that England has not produced any
notable experimental poetry (this being the domain, apparently, of the Welsh
and Scots). Roy Fisher? Peter Redgrove? Peter Reading? Denise Riley? Peter Riley?
It's true that poets of an experimental bent, of the kind represented in the
Crozier/Longville anthology, can return the exclusivist compliment, but it seems
a pity to be locked within another binary opposition, condemned always to sup
from only side of the table.

One of the useful things the book does is to position the experience of war as
central to the twentieth century, but also to the development of its poetry. Few
could argue against the claim that 'Modernity in its guise as modern war has

profoundly reshaped poetry', yet often poets whose work has been profoundly shaped by the experience of war have been confined to anthologies of war poetry. Longley performs a useful and important service by incorporating poets like Ivor Gurney, Isaac Rosenberg, Alun Lewis, Henry Reed and Keith Douglas into her vision of the century's poetry. The experience of war and the memory of war is a part of the work of many poets represented here who would not normally be thought of as 'war poets', from Larkin to Hughes and Fenton, as well as Heaney, Mahon, Michael Longley, Muldoon and Carson. She reads the relative neglect of the poets of the world wars as a further sign of the depredations visited on poetry by the champions of modernism, certain critics tending to find them conservative or reactionary. You sometimes get the feeling that Longley would be a lot happier if 'The Waste Land' had been written somewhere else, in another language.

Although the *Bloodaxe Book* is an anthology of poetry produced in these islands, some bits of the archipelago seem a shade under-represented. Besides Paul Durcan and and Eiléan Ní Chuilleanáin, poetry from the Republic of Ireland since the sixties does not figure. A book that claims Ian Duhig and Jo Shapcott as 'key' poets of the century might, you would have thought, have found room for Thomas Kinsella, Richard Murphy, Michael Hartnett, Thomas McCarthy or Eavan Boland. Nor is there any sign of a Welsh poet after the two Thomases. Robert Minhinnick, Gillian Clarke and Menna Elfyn are absent. Scotland fares a bit better. It's good to see Edwin Morgan, Robert Garioch, Kathleen Jamie and Don Paterson, though I could have done with more W.S. Graham and it seems odd that no room could be found for either Robert Crawford or W.N. Herbert. But these are endless arguments and are of interest to few, I suspect, besides the compilers and the excluded, who could go on trading griefs and reasons until doomsday. As a serviceable anthology of some of the best English-language poetry produced in these islands in the last centrury, this is a good book, and as good a place to start as any; as an argument, though, the book is as stubbornly partial as any of the other anthologies its editor rebukes.

＊

Poets and critics will always disagree about aesthetics and traditions; it's the nature of the business. The extent to which literary and cultural/political debates overlap in Ireland lends these kinds of discussions an urgency they would be unlikely to have elsewhere. The new pamphlet series 'Crosscurrents', published by Cork University Press in association with the Centre for Cross-Border Studies in Armagh, again illustrates the binarism that is an inescapable fact of debate on this island. *Multi-Culturalism: The View from the Two Irelands* is a head-to-head in which Longley and Declan Kiberd articulate their senses of the different, and opposing, directions of the two societies.

Longley starts from the view that Ireland has been locked in a *Kulturkampf* between two mono-cultural societies for a hundred and fifty years, and she asks: 'how can we make our differences fruitful?' Any notion of integration is premature in the resolutely divided society of Northern Ireland, and 'A few years of peace process will not quickly change settlement patterns or social patterns produced by thirty years of civil war.' Her reading of the present situation is fairly bleak. She's critical of the kind of minimalist multi-culturalism that focuses exclusively on the right of each culture to cherish its difference. And, on the other hand, she's critical of the Republic for what she sees as its failure to comprehend Northern Ireland; the tigerish Republic has, she feels, advanced so far down its own secularizing and materialist path that it is actually less able than ever to accommodate unionism. She quotes the Archdeacon of Dublin, Gordon Linney, who recently expressed 'growing unease at the apparent drift of elements in the political establishment in the South towards a nationalist/ republican alliance with a dated political agenda which by its very nature excludes modern unionism'. Longley's view of this is that a new 'soft-focus' Irishness has replaced ideological nationalism and revisionism with a bland acceptance of the nationalist agenda. Unionism is met with, at best, indifference.

She may be right in that the new Ireland is not overly given to self-questioning and is daily less interested in the competing ideologies of nationalism and unionism. This is undoubtedly matched by Northern indifference to or incomprehension of the directions in which the Republic is headed. She may take too literally the self-congratulatory rhetoric that fills the air in the Republic, and may underestimate the rapidity with which this state is changing and has changed already – it may be symptomatic of this that Declan Kiberd's companion piece addresses racism, immigration and multi-culturalism largely in terms of the recent experience of the Republic, and only briefly deals with Northern Ireland. When he does, he proposes that both communities need to 'seek freedom within a multi-cultural community'. Longley's vision of multi-culturalism depends on the breakdown of the existing 'monoculturalisms'. The Republic, she feels, will have to question its 'conceptual infrastructure', be prepared to yield cultural and political sovereignty; nationalists and unionists will have to be impelled towards each other by the governments. She sees hope in a strong and distinct sense of Northernness within 'a more Scandinavian concept of the archipelago', a civic and cultural entity with its own internal coherence and interesting sets of relationships with the surrounding entities. It's a concept that has informed her critical vision from the outset, and it will take another couple of generations to test the strength of 'a European region where you can live in three places at once (Ireland/Britain/"Ulster")'. By then, as she suggests, the whole of Europe may have come to resemble Northern Ireland.

EDNA LONGLEY, *Poetry & Posterity*, Tarset: Bloodaxe Books.

EDNA LONGLEY, ed., *The Bloodaxe Book of 20th Century Poetry*, Tarset: Bloodaxe Books.

EDNA LONGLEY AND DECLAN KIBERD, *Multi-Culturalism: The View from the Two Irelands*, Cork: Cork University Press in association with the Centre for Cross-Border Studies, Armagh (series editor: Andy Pollak).

Here, now

MOLLY MCCLOSKEY

Out here, where home is – 12 miles from town, 132 from the capital, latitude 54 degrees 20 minutes, longitude 8 degrees 40 – we're at the centre of our universe. Our peninsula: tiny feline tongue-flick into the endless liquid of the Atlantic. *Cape Neurotic, breakaway republic, bandit country* – all pet names, only the first of which I've ever understood. Much further north and you're AWOL, into the too-high wilds of Donegal. But here, despite the silence, we seem not too far from anywhere. Silence that sometimes – like a climber's nightmare, a hidden cleft – feels like the firm earth having suddenly given way beneath us, dropping us irretrievably into dark and hollow. Only an illusion; we're on solid ground here. Nestled between mountain and shoreline, or rise and fall, able anytime to look left, or right, and be shown what it is we're relative to.

From where we are (as from a lot of places now), the new highways radiate like spokes from the hub we imagine *here* is, drilling past the now redundant, serpentine old laneways (recall: the shock of rod and spiral, side-by-side on the small slide, your very first turn at the microscope). Suggestion of stark choice, between what demands but rewards, and the line of least resistance. Roads hastening us in three directions, towards Galway, Dublin, Donegal. Roads referred to not by name but by order of appearance: Old and New. As though there would only ever be two versions of a thing, or ever one definitive account.

SUMMER

Reneged-on promise, spring's failure to deliver, *coitus interruptus* of a season. Worse somehow than winter, which, at the very least, arrives. I haven't learned it, the fine art of pessimism. How to stop expecting. *Teach me,* she wrote, before departing, *what I have to have to live in this country.**

*Jean Valentine, from 'Fellini in Purgatory'

THE NEW ROAD

Which you and I didn't live to see. Lying in your upstairs bedroom all that dank summer of its construction, its tripartite beat tripping off our tongues. Eight-point-eight kilometres of sudden superhighway and right outside your door. The changes it would bring! As though it were the coming of the motor-car itself. Here to there in no time flat; what we couldn't do with a proper passing lane. How what for eons had been villages would overnight begin to feel like 'suburbs'. We hadn't much else to talk about, which doesn't mean they weren't good nights.

Autumn, and someone else by then. Talk of the highway assumes the present tense. The local paper runs a front-page piece on how to navigate a roundabout. The Sunday drive assumes proportions it never dreamed of. A *dual carriageway*. Could the term be any more charming, or less appropriate? And each time a new one opens, we shave minutes off the trip to Dublin. As if through some polite willingness on our part to illustrate a proof of plate tectonics, we inch ever closer to the capital.

THE OLD ROAD

Despite my love of speed and the queer way that vast, industrial swath through the scree appealed to me, when coming to you I stuck instead to the old road. With its bad bends, its fog banks, its stray cows come upon round corners and our own agreement that the new way was far less arduous, the old nevertheless maintained a coy hold on my loyalty. As though to remind me of where I'd come from, or of the condition in which I'd first arrived at your door. Slow and inefficient, knotted.

The old road bearing the weight and imprint of all those winter nights I travelled to and from you. Who I was, or who you were, on any given Friday. My stabs at perpetuity. My way of saying I'll keep returning to wherever you are, somehow the same, somehow fortified against change, against age and the flux of season and the occasional fit of pique. My way of knowing that we have been here, again and again, at your huge hearth at the end of each workweek, swapping laconically the details of our lives. Who you pined for, or who I did. Long-distance liaisons. Sound advice. Constancy and repetition and yet the bloom of things too. For laconic as we were, we were not immune to wonder, imagining we saw our very souls ripen under the watchful eyes of time and mutual regard.

HERE

At dawn or on summer evenings, the landscape an inversion of itself, things assuming their complementary colours: a yellow sky; Benbulben, which I know to be green, now a deep magenta. Five hundred twenty-six metres high and always there, in its uncanny self-possession, its horizontal thrust, its air of presumption and demand. Depending on the light, the angle, my own mood: priapic jut, or extended arm ushering me in, and northward. And to the south, its other: dome to its mantel, afloat while it is all full steam ahead. Self-satisfied, too, but afterwards, and in repose. Flat on its back and pooling like an ample breast.

PARKING DISCS

To the introduction of which nothing definitive could be attributed. Not the end of an era, not the mark of our entry into the grown-up world of cineplexes, bottle banks, espresso bars and, yes, the sex shop. But something. A kind of attrition.

In the beginning, we parked in cul-de-sacs or on the outskirts. Or we cheated – 'recycled' – carefully arranging on the dash hair squeegies, ballpoint pens or cigarette lighters over the already scratched squares of our tattered parking discs. We swapped tips on hidden spaces, as though they were undiscovered holiday destinations. (That private lot smack in the centre of town, some still-virgin corner of the world.) Gradually, though, we gave in. Learned to plan ahead. Bought in bulk packets of ten, and forgot there was ever a time when we didn't have to pay to park.

The papers say we are living in a boom town, and we feel it. We feel that weird, too-quick reversal of decay. And each time something picturesque and tumbledown vanishes and something baby blue or canary yellow or forest green rises in its place, we sense the presence of allegory. Allegory is among the words we don't much use here, but we know enough to know when it's among us. Each time we forget what once existed in any given place, we are visited by a vague unease, as though we have colluded in some dubious scientific advance.

BEFORE ...

and in the company of some other you. Platonic too, but with whom so many roles were played. Who's lost, who's found, first me, then you. So that I'm waiting, uneasily, for the next reversal. Or better yet, the final incarnation of us: some sync finally fallen into, a place – on the far shore – where suspicion's banished, ethanol extinct, and gratitude so deep-ingrained it isn't necessary to refer to.

That Christmas – our cold hands calcifying round our wine glasses in the icy studio of some mutual artist friend – we clung to one another in the corner like a pair of co-dependent limpets, guffawing over my latest half-remembered scrape, and you had the backhanded good grace to say to me: *There's a good woman going to loss in there.* Two years later, some early-morning stint in your place, the heebie-jeebies now a spectator sport to me, and I'm trying hard to say the same to you – a good man – because it's true. Because I never have, and still can't.

IARNRÓD ÉIREANN

In the bathroom on the Sligo–Dublin railway line, a sign telling us how to turn on the water in the hand basin has been tampered with, so as to form a new message – the demanding, unheralded art of negative graffiti. Whole words scratched out, one 's' artfully obscured, and what we're left with is an in-joke with a world-view attached. Think of here: the affection with which ineptitude is regarded, the irony with which piety is infused. When visiting from abroad, if short on time and desiring to grasp this place in a soundbite, you might start here: *To obtain water ... pray.*

WHICH BRINGS US TO BORN-AGAIN VIRGINS

A mini-movement growing up on the far side of the Atlantic: recant your past carnality, reclaim your prelapsarian self. A sort of sexual face-lift. This news courtesy of Radio Telefís Éireann, and relayed with all the ill-suppressed mirth that such American hokum incites. Some weeks later (also via RTÉ, though now with quizzicality in place of mirth), this news: that the Pioneers are offering a deal. Temperance, they've decided, can start anytime. Even here, it's not about never anymore. Just two years without a drink and you too can wear the pin, be, as it were, born again. The brands of innocence we consider worth regaining. A juxtaposing that helplessly invites reduction: *the difference between us is ...* that we dream of re-imagining our sex lives; you, of alcoholic chastity.

... AFTER

That I could hand to you – *a good man*, after all – the rebirth of wonder. The chastening effect of mental clarity, emotional acuity, keenness of sensation. Strictly *bona fide* fear. In a word (so hackneyed it hurts), sobriety. No longer awash in that amniotic fluid. See it shaken from you, like excess sea water upon emerging, the evolutionary being that is you heeding an unconscious call to a next echelon. Or your own tide out, brackishness receded, detritus exposed, the dropped hints of your life – *still there* – marking the way back. Equivocal treasures you'd glean then, ugly only to the untrained eye, like the bleached skulls we see on other people's mantels, prized beyond reason for reasons other than themselves.

My Christmas list for you: an undiluted consciousness, the prickliness and nettle-itch of fresh idea, pins and needles – this time – of boyish awe, the eager jump-start of each early morning, a mind you could strike a match on. If I could see it through sufficiently, to the point where I can say I haven't failed you. To the naff soda pops and the too-much smoking. To the living gingerly, the chaperoned existence, the life as though in kid gloves. To the graceful retirement of the anti-hero and the point of diminishing returns. Not only reached, but recognized.

NOW

In a parking lot somewhere in New Jersey, amidst a sea of stickered bumpers (declarations of intent, pithy quips, statements of preference), one-stop wisdom shop of the New World –

There are many vacancies in the motel of your mind.
Handguns in schools: for or against?
And marvellously: *I'd rather be sailing to Byzantium*

– there in the land of mobility and reinvention, simulation and submerged rebirthing, alien abduction and impregnation, of wishful thinking never content to remain so, one radical assertion of intransigence stands out, a lone (ironic) voice sagely, trenchantly satisfied with its lot:

I'd rather be here, now.

HOME

Always when off the train. And at just that spot. Someone said it's hard to leave here because of that configuration of mountain and shoreline. The curvature of one along the other and the way we're lodged between. Concentric vortex of an embrace, poisoned chalice, gift tax.

But always on returning from the capital it hits, the bashfulness that too much generosity inspires. Summer evenings especially, coming west by train. Three hours of hell, then … *Carrick-on-Shannon, Boyle, Ballymote, Collooney* … and knowing it's coming, finding it there, stepping down onto the platform, a sort of guilty glee, as though I've skipped with the booty and this is it: being here. That strangely subterranean feel to the place, to being this little bit beyond the pale and harbouring the secret of where a thing is hid.

Into the car then, down, down the hill and out of town, into the deepening quiet and the thickening dark, spelunking my way towards home. The same chagrin at my own dumb joy and just when I'm wondering what's behind it, it's there, in front of me, curving into view. That overly invoked mountain that two days ago I couldn't get shut of fast enough, over my shoulder everywhere I went, like a cheap dick on my tail, always *there*, in whatever ham disguise: pink, green, black, cut cake, 2-D cut-out, tidal wave, hung curtain, bad landscape painting, noun demanding adjectival range I haven't got. But now, seeing it afresh, I'm brought to heel, as corny as it feels. Just there. At Rathcormack, with the mountain on my right, the bay on my left, and that water-slide of a road, easing me into home. The plink of hit water. My own silent shout of delight.

... WELL AS WELL HIM AS ANOTHER ...

or so it pays to pretend. Until such time, anyway, as the clear truth of its antithesis can be admitted: that parts, while consecutive, are by no means interchangeable. That a hierarchy of affection exists – complete with petty power struggle, cut deal, bloodless coup, the tenterhook of dominion near-divested, and the pathos of the monarch unaware of plot-simmer – theocratic or despotic or with the mind-bending intricacy of the most bloated bureaucracy, but never, ever populist.

And always, long afterwards, the one we still talk about, the golden age of whatever our private civilization's been.

You? But could I ever know this before the end? Before all theory's been tested and each variable assigned value. The temptation to believe some untried proof remains.

If I'm even asking, it probably isn't you.

But your way of going on, like life was a game you'd deigned to play. Rather graciously, rather indulgently, all things considered (though granted, with an underlying gravity). Your figurative pose: winsomely awkward adult seated lotus-like in front of some board game with pretty coloured pieces and squares you can't afford to land on. Eager player, player by whatever wacky handed-down rules, consulter of box top when arbitrating chaos – kids' favourite bachelor uncle – but angling all the time to divine the grand design, the blackly comic hand of the creator (Milton-Bradley©) obvious to you at every turn. You've it sussed, you at your two levels, but to your credit aren't pretending you're not thoroughly engaged. Or that you don't know your place; fetchingly – as relatively in the dark as anyone – you aren't above availing of kid-wisdom.

Some near-future, when I can take you with a grain of salt, stop concocting overblown metaphors for your existence. My fantasies now reduced to those of resignation, dead nerves, you having worn yourself thin. Once, though, it was like what I've heard of heroin: like being kissed by God. So I'm counting on the flat affect to follow. But that image won't hold up; your grip on me will loosen, after all. To the point where it's work to want you; already (sometimes), something more than simply waking is required. And after that – I hope – I'll find you there. But without the power to call up anything at all in me other than that old sardonic warmth. And I will wax eloquent for you on the matter of my latest object of desire, your by now banal presence reminding me that he – like you, like all my other little gods – will fall.

... ANOTHER

Our first touch, the coy plucking of insects off of one another's sleeves.

Oh, and you've one too. Here, let me ...

Days earlier, before we'd even spoken, I'd sat three rows behind you in a half-full theatre, imagining your hand through your hair was my own. Following your attention to where it wandered. Feeling cooler when you shed your coat. Smiling when you looked left to display, for my benefit, your profile. I thought I felt you squirm under the creaturely scent-sniff of my gaze and suddenly liked you, very much, for submitting so civilly to my inspection.

Later, when I referred to it, you surprised me by claiming that the whole mute exchange had been only in my mind. But I'm less convinced than ever.

Your way of being, once I knew you, only confirming my suspicions. You were rare that way, how you could sit back and be enjoyed. Almost – I hate to say it – *female*, the way you gave yourself. Stealing the show like that: all object. I get it finally, the slavish love of beauty. The need to keep you in my sightline, and at my fingertips. The way, like an animal, I squirreled away sensations, stockpiling them for the cold spell to come.

LOVE AND MARRIAGE

In the kitchen of some too-long-married couple I know, I see they've retiled the walls. Over dinner, they conduct a tête-à-tête of injury and insult, the text from which they're working so highly allusive the rest of us can only hum along. We're all waiting for the split, for the relief of it. I, in fact, am betting they won't see next week. But then I think about their kitchen. The forward march of it. The things people do when we aren't around. Plugging away like that. Piling brick on brick. Surprising us with the way they keep rising from their deathbeds.

SOLIPSISM

Or a distant cousin of. Conundrum of unrequited love: that there is nothing so unlikely to arouse my sympathy or interest as your (unreciprocated) ardour for me. When what should please me more than passing hours in your company, pondering your unshakeable faith in my splendidness? Pining alongside you even, as we gaze into the near distance together, our four eyes trained on that superlative creature we've agreed is *I*. I – and I transformed by you like every other routine, workaday object when seen through your presently narcotized eyes – should be the sole subject of which I never tire.

So how is it instead that what I feel is pawed? I love you, after all, just not *that* way. How is it then that your own love sits between us like an intrusive third party? A crasher at our table, a morose drunk, a mourner who's so far exceeded the limits of our sympathy as to arouse resentment. Injecting into our otherwise gay little soirée the end of fun, a parental call to order, the killjoy knell of schoolbells, dawn. I watch, helplessly, as myself is extracted from myself. Yolk from white. Or decanted and given back to me as dregs, while you hold on to what's finest. You say I have 'taken possession' of you and yet it is I who feel owned. Where have I gone? And how can I give back to you the gift of indifference, the same indifference I once worked so hard to overcome?

Thankfully, this tells me something. That the anguish I myself am so enjoying (over someone other than you) will never – however stubbornly it tries – create something where there is nothing. This is how I'm able to believe what beggars belief: that while I have not for one full minute failed to think of him, or performed one interior monologue but for *him* to hear, or sat still *anywhere* but that I envisioned his smiling, inexplicable entrance (never mind the fact he's out of town, out of the country, has never heard of here, and doesn't drive anyway), I – like some out-of-the-way eatery he often forgets exists – have not even occurred to him tonight.

This is how I learn the necessity of giving up, through this grown-up game of Pass the Parcel.

'RAPTURE'

Which I first heard while sitting on your porch. That screened-in affair which seemed suspended in mid-air, the way it jutted out over a mini-valley, the path cut through the trees unfurling underneath us. The constant rain, the always saturated earth, the vertiginousness of our perch, and the delicate discordancy of *Thirteen Harmonies*.

We felt straight out of *Deliverance*.

Ice melting. Or that was what you called it. Falling apart, it felt like. And then later, watching, as I failed to fall apart.

I'm thinking of a scavenger hunt, a game I used to love, and the list I'd need to help me find you: John Cage, Dusty Springfield, the Ford dealership on 202, resourcefulness, your own love of lists, that shade of blue, your spot-on send-up of the Stage Manager in *Our Town*, the library and the field beside – alive each night with lightning bugs, living by your wits, your own regained wonder (after the 'intervening years of anaesthetization'), bicycles, Bonnard, a sleek black lap-top, and 1:26 of 'Rapture'.

CHRISTMAS

Dinner and a long walk through Dromahair. Blatantly storybook, with winding lane, lone spire perforating mist, duskiness congealing too quickly into night, and we seven – gloved and hatted – trudging smally through the stock-still hills. Barnacle geese in the marshy field, wintering here before their spring coupling elsewhere. And of humans? All with me in pairs, all six snug aboard the ark. Sweet platonic friendships I could frankly do without; company, under the cir-cumstances, always worse than solitude. At home, at least, I've my familiars – undemanding silence, ritual of book and bed, arch-backed animal rising sleepily at the sound of my key turning – sticks to beat self-pity down. Self-pity, that rav-enous ingrate that rises balefully at the simple act of 'bucking up' for company. Uninvited guest grossly feeding on itself. Asexual reproducer gone berserk, begetting and begetting with no apparent need for outside intervention (though the hospitality of friends will do nicely). Touch Socratic even, in its arrogance, how it runs rings round what I'm absolutely sure is reason.

But there's no reasoning with now. This time of year is cruel, and makes glar-ing all our lacks. You gone by then, and like a ghost beside me. You are anyone by now, though, and what's glaring is your very lack of specificity. An absence generic as a presence never could be, though on the side of each this much could be said: if present, possibility personified; if absent, failure of same.

This year's lesson: that loneliness, like a sick cell, will reinvent itself. Mutate, strengthen, grow resistant to the old remedies. That there are strains I haven't even dreamed of.

INCANTATION,

prayer at bedtime, Angelus for the secular set.

From Malin Head to Howth Head to the Irish Sea.

Swaddled in my bed, quick listen to the news, just before lights out, just checking: was there anything that happened I should know about?

From Carnsore Point to Valentia to Erris Head.

Sudden sense of smallness, shelter and inclusion. The fact that weather can be met, across the board, with only silence. Incongruous comfort of our collective ineffectuality – the few limits we do share. Why winter has always seemed the most communal of seasons. How death stymies – then binds – the living, levelling who's left as well.

From Erris Head to Belfast Lough to Hook Head.

Quiet pang of guilt. For what? For being here. Cosseted by airwaves, by four walls from the audible wind, warm, dry, safe and, really, OK. For the dumb good luck then of being here, which on the best days seems surely a remarkable omission, or oversight.

Rosslare. Roche's Point Automatic. Valentia. Belmullet … 999 steady … 996 and rising slowly … Loop Head. Mizen Head. Carnsore Point. And on the Irish Sea.

Never more foreign than now. And yet, on hearing, of all things, the Sea Area Forecast, never since a child this tucked-in sensation. Crack of light under the door and life going on beyond it. Someone out there, with an eye on things. Parameters delineated. The compass-points of home. To be told where I am, and what bound by. Like the child's incantation. Universe: galaxy: solar system: planet: hemisphere: continent: nation: state: city: street …

… HOME

Out the back, a biopsy of *here*. Field, hill and dale. Copse, the spire at Lissadell, hunkered shrubs cordoning off holdings, red-roofed barns and one stark white bungalow. The mountain – robbed at twilight of its contours – now a prow on the horizon. Through the keyhole view I'm given – this lens eye – pan here, then here, pull back, wide angle now, see a country echo in concentric rings of just this. Or fly over it. All like a doll's house, down to diminutive detail, and knowable, you think, in one crossing. The human scale of things. The illusion therefore that you can grasp it. Learn the one thing you need to live here.

TOURISM

Moon over the back sheds on ink-blue nights. A rusty bike and wagon wheel propped against the side stone wall. The sheds, just shells of things. You see them everywhere. Candidates for conversion. But I like them roofless. The way the gable ends stand, regardless, as if holding up their end of the bargain. Every so often – out of the blue and never when I seek the thrill – it broadsides me, this scene in silhouette. I stare, like a tourist, into relative prehistory.

And you, living in the shadow of that old abbey. When I'd asked and you'd told me – 1508, offhandedly – I was silenced. Centuries still strike me dumb, no matter what I learn, just keep seeming beyond my ken. As though I'm all jig time, quik-stop, planned obsolescence. What's coming, rather than what's gone.

Constellations, first here, now here. The stars obscured for weeks by cloud cover and suddenly it breaks, and like the automated flick from one slide in the carousel to the next: a new view. Over and over, the strobing of the night sky. I step outside before bed and look up. Sometimes, even on the clearest nights: *nothing*: my own laziness of heart. A guilty inability to rise to the occasion. Sometimes, though, an awe that seems almost equal to the sight. A wholeness and no complaint. The *knowing*. And the not fearing not knowing.

THE HALE-BOPP

Zany name for what hung over us that summer, as though to keep us from taking miracle too seriously. Sounding to me like a dance my mother might have done forty-some years ago. Jiving at a mixer in West Philly. It used to hover, suspended dead centre above the straight stretch of the Donegal Road. And I, driving north, each time with the illusion of drawing nearer to it.

You then too. There with me and eye trained skyward, you. Not another, not yet fallen nor ever will be. But with me. Two of us then, standing, with our simple mouths agape and my heart gone out to us. In that prolonged instant of afforded joy, in which the eye-blink of wish-time was arrested. When we stood, you and I there, in a state of continuous grace, under that one always falling star which finally, that September, fell from view.

12 O'Clock News

gooseneck lamp

As you all know, tonight is the night of the full moon, half the world over. But here the moon seems to hang motionless in the sky. It gives very little light; it could be dead. Visibility is poor. Nevertheless, we shall try to give you some idea of the lay of the land and the present situation.

typewriter

The escarpment that rises abruptly from the central plain is in heavy shadow, but the elaborate terracing of its southern glacis gleams faintly in the dim light, like fish scales. What endless labor those small, peculiarly shaped terraces represent! And yet, on them the welfare of this tiny principality depends.

pile of mss.

A slight landslide occurred in the northwest about an hour ago. The exposed soil appears to be of poor quality: almost white, calcareous, and shaly. There are believed to have been no casualties.

typed sheet

Almost due north, our aerial reconnaissance reports the discovery of a large rectangular "field," hitherto unknown to us, obviously man-made. It is dark-speckled. An airstrip? A cemetery?

envelopes

In this small, backward country, one of the most backward left in the world today, communications are crude and "industrialization" and its products almost nonexistent. Strange to say, however, signboards are on a truly gigantic scale.

We have also received reports of a mysterious, oddly shaped, black structure, at an undisclosed distance to the east. Its presence was revealed only because its highly polished surface catches such feeble moonlight as prevails. The natural resources of the country being far from completely known to us, there is the possibility that this may be, or may contain, some powerful and terrifying "secret weapon." On the other hand, given what we *do* know, or have learned from our anthropologists and sociologists about this people, it may well be nothing more than a *numen*, or a great altar recently erected to one of their gods, to which, in their present historical state of superstition and helplessness, they attribute magical powers, and may even regard as a "savior," one last hope of rescue from their grave difficulties.

ink-bottle

At last! One of the elusive natives has been spotted! He appears to be — rather, to have been — a unicyclist-courier, who may have met his end by falling from the height of the escarpment because of the deceptive illumination. Alive, he would have been small, but undoubtedly proud and erect, with the thick, bristling black hair typical of the indigenes.

typewriter eraser

From our superior vantage point, we can clearly see into a sort of dugout, possibly a shell crater, a "nest" of soldiers. They lie heaped together, wearing the camouflage "battle dress" intended for "winter warfare." They are in hideously contorted positions, all dead. We can make out at least eight bodies. These uniforms were designed to be used in guerrilla warfare on the country's one snow-covered mountain peak. The fact that these poor soldiers are wearing them *here*, on the plain, gives further proof, if proof were necessary, either of the childishness and hopeless impracticality of this inscrutable people, our opponents, or of the sad corruption of their leaders.

ashtray

ELIZABETH BISHOP

'The harbor is always a mess'

PAUL MULDOON

The following essay was delivered, in slightly different form, as a lecture on 31 October 2000 at Oxford University, where Paul Muldoon is Professor of Poetry. It is part of a series of lectures entitled 'The End of the Poem'.

One aspect of the phrase 'The End of the Poem' which I plan to consider here is that of the delineation of where verse ends and prose begins, a delineation somewhat blurred, if not obliterated, by the mode of the 'prose poem'. I'm reminded of the dangers and difficulties attending such a project by Robert Giroux's account, in his introduction to her *Collected Prose*, of his first meeting with Elizabeth Bishop:

> She was an extremely attentive listener, but scarcely spoke until I told her of my experience escorting Marianne Moore to the New York première of T.S. Eliot's *The Cocktail Party*, at his request (he was unable to leave London). After the performance, we had been caught in the aisle behind the Duke of Windsor, and heard him say (at which point Marianne poked me gently in the ribs): 'They tell me Mr. Eliot wrote this play in verse, but I'd say you'd *never* know it!'

It was Eliot himself, of course, who had weighed in on the subject of verse and prose in his 1917 *New Statesman* article on 'The Borderline of Prose':

> Both verse and prose still conceal unexplored possibilities, but whatever one writes must be definitely and by inner necessity either one or the other.

While Eliot wrote at least one magnificent prose poem – I'm thinking of 'Hysteria' – he was inclined to dislike, even to disallow, the term, all too aware that the borderline between verse and prose represented by the form was a minefield in which any hard and fast theory would almost certainly be exploded. In my musings on this subject, I'll also try to be mindful of the view of Owen Barfield, also expressed in an article in the *New Statesman*, this time in 1928, that 'to regard concentrations on hybrids or borderline cases as a means of clearing up typical differences' is mistaken:

> Whereas in point of fact these borderline cases are the most likely ones of all to confuse our minds, inducing us to ask the wrong kind of questions, and to forget what we are inquiring for in the ardour of inquiry.

That Elizabeth Bishop's prose poem '12 O'Clock News' might itself be concerned with such 'borderline cases' is suggested by the fourth paragraph/stanza, which describes a '*typed sheet*' as a 'field' that is 'dark-speckled' and 'obviously man-made'.* The poem asks us to think of the '*typed sheet*' as being akin to an 'airstrip' or 'cemetery'. I suppose that, in the overall context of the landscape of the writer's desk described in the prose poem, this typewritten page may itself be seen as either a rough and ready runway, a clearing dotted with tree-stumps, or, more persuasively, a cemetery covered with makeshift signs, the crossings-out of a work in progress. Within the smaller context of the '*typed sheet*' itself, the white expanses of the page margins, or the breaks between verse-stanzas or prose-paragraphs, are more likely to substantiate the 'airstrip' than the 'cemetery' interpretation. There is, in any event, the positing of a relationship between topography and typography. Some of you may recall that, in my attempt to read Robert Frost's 'The Mountain', I was much concerned with any number of 'blanks' in the poem, including the exaggerated stanza breaks in its typographical presentation. There I appealed briefly to Ralph Waldo Emerson's 1836 essay on 'Nature' to try to make sense of one reading of those 'blanks' in

*'12 O'Clock News' is printed in its entirety on pp. 92–93, with kind permission of Farrar, Straus and Giroux.

the 'ruin or the blank that we see when we look at nature'. I might also have appealed to Emerson for the provenance – or part of the provenance – of line eight of 'The Mountain', which reads 'When I walked forth at dawn to see new things'. In his essay 'The Poet', published in book form in 1844, Emerson writes:

> For it is not metres, but a metre-making argument, that makes a poem – a thought so passionate and alive that like the spirit of a plant or animal it has an architecture of its own, and adorns nature with a new thing.

I suspect that the spirit of Emerson's 'new thing' lies somewhat behind the title of '12 O'Clock News', as do, more substantially, Ezra Pound's paired maxims that 'literature is news that stays news' and that a poet must 'make it new'. This last injunction of Pound also lies somewhat behind Bishop's description of the 'field' as 'hitherto unknown to us', or 'new'. The phrase 'obviously man-made' refers directly to a 'poem', I expect, since a 'man-made' thing would be the outcome of the activity described by the Greek word *poiesis*. The objective of the poem itself to make metaphors (to find likeness in unlike things, to present, in the Emersonian sense, new ways of seeing the things of the world), is another aspect of the phrase 'The End of the Poem' I'd like to try to explore here. Yet another sense of the phrase I'll be focusing on, in my passes over the terrain of this prose poem, is that of the precise location of the surface of the poem, particularly where there seems to be a discrepancy between the surface and the subterranean – what we generally term 'irony'. Along the way, I'll attempt to place '12 O'Clock News' in the context of some of Elizabeth Bishop's other writing, not only the poems appearing with it in her last collection, *Geography III*, a book that came out in 1976, three years before her death in 1979, but also some of her prose writings, including one or two of her other prose poems. I'll also say a brief word or two about the impact of this prose poem on three or four subsequent writers of poetry and prose, including Seamus Heaney, Derek Mahon, Craig Raine and Salman Rushdie.

*

I used the word 'margins' just a moment ago, and I'll come back to it now and linger over it a little while, not least because the notion of the margin, not to speak of the marginal, is particularly relevant to '12 O'Clock News'. We notice that the body of the text is justified right, the conventional justification for prose, prose that springs forward rather than verse that falls back. The text is also justified left, of course, but with a much wider 'airstrip' than usual running down the side of the page. This allows for an italicized legend on the left of the page – '*typed sheet*', say – to point, like an anatomical term connected by an invisible arrow to a feature of the main body of the text on the right:

> Almost due north, our aerial reconnaissance reports the discovery of a large rectangular "field," hitherto unknown to us, obviously man-made. It is dark-speckled. An airstrip? A cemetery?

By the time we've read this, we're already familiar with the process of defamiliarization in which the poem exults, so familiar indeed that we may have jumped a little ahead of ourselves and concentrated on the left-hand monitor, or stereophonic speaker, and got the bass-line of the poem from that series of italicized 'legends' – '*gooseneck lamp*', '*typewriter*', '*pile of mss.*', '*typed sheet*', '*envelopes*', '*ink-bottle*', '*typewriter eraser*', and '*ashtray*'. These are not only things of the world but things of a writer's world, the view of, and from, a writer's desk which, as I've already mentioned, may be said to be the 'subject' of '12 O'Clock News'. One can imagine a circumstance in which this left-hand column might be seen as revealing too much, a circumstance in which we prefer to read the 'answer' at the back of the book, or even upside down at the bottom of the page, rather than have it given simultaneously with, if not a little before, the question. Part of the delight, surely, of trying to make sense of a riddle from the *Exeter Book* lies in our not quite knowing what is being described. Is it a bird? Is it a plane? Is it a gooseneck lamp? Such questions are irrelevant, it would seem, when we know straight away that it is most definitely a *'gooseneck lamp'*. That the poem is concerned with this tension between knowing and unknowing is evident from the outset since the promise of 'News' in the title is immediately contradicted by the opening words of the poem, at once buttonholing and blasé:

> As you all know, tonight is the night of the full moon, half the world over. But here the moon seems to hang motionless in the sky. It gives very little light; it could be dead. Visibility is poor. Nevertheless, we shall try to give you some idea of the lay of the land and the present situation.

It will become clear, as the poem proceeds, that Bishop's primary aim here is to mix and match – not necessarily smoothly and seamlessly, for reasons I'll come to later – three or four types of discourse. They are those of the anthropologist or sociologist ('it may well be nothing more than a *numen*, or a great altar recently erected to one of their gods'), the travel writer ('At last! One of the elusive natives has been spotted!'), the foreign, or war, correspondent ('There are believed to have been no casualties') and, allied to this last, the radio or television reporter ('we shall try to give you some idea of the lay of the land and the present situation'). The discourse of the television report is particularly significant in this respect since it accounts, at least partly, for the provenance of what I referred to earlier as the 'legends' to the left of the page, which might be much more usefully viewed as 'captions', or 'titles', or 'idents' on a television screen. The description, in the eighth paragraph/stanza of '12 O'Clock News', of the *'ashtray'* full of soldiers in 'hideously contorted positions, all dead' owes something of its immediacy to television reportage of the Vietnam war, that most immediate, most media-mediated, of conflicts, which had finally come to some sort of end in 1975, the year before '12 O'Clock News' was collected. In so far as anything may be said to come naturally to a writer, the discourse of the television report of this era must have come fairly naturally to Elizabeth Bishop, since its

features of clarity, conciseness and concreteness, combined with a certain cool-
ness (in the sense of editorial detachment), had been the hall- or watermarks of
her poetry from the very beginning. Writing in *The Nation* of her first collection,
North & South, which appeared in 1946, Marianne Moore had observed:

> Elizabeth Bishop is spectacular in being unspectacular. Why has no one
> ever thought of this, one asks oneself; why not be accurate and modest?

Moore knows of one or two poets who have 'thought of this', of course, as is evident from her allusion to the structure and substance of a celebrated sentence
from Edward Thomas's celebrated review, one of three he wrote in quick suc-
cession, of Robert Frost's *North of Boston*:

> These poems are revolutionary because they lack the exaggeration of
> rhetoric, and even at first sight appear to lack the poetic intensity of
> which rhetoric is an imitation.

As we know to be so often the case with writers' comments on other writers,
the insight Thomas offers into Frost's poetic practice affords an even greater
insight into his own. In Thomas's 'Cock-Crow', for example, one can see, in the
first seven lines, a mimicking of 'the exaggeration of rhetoric' to which he
refers:

> Out of the wood of thoughts that grows by night
> To be cut down by the sharp axe of light, –
> Out of the night, two cocks together crow,
> Cleaving the darkness with a silver blow:
> And bright before my eyes twin trumpeters stand,
> Heralds of splendour, one at either hand,
> Each facing each as in a coat of arms:

The eighth, and final, line of the poem would appear, in Thomas's phrase, 'to lack poetic intensity':

The milkers lace their boots up at the farms.

The tension between lines seven and eight of 'Cock-Crow', the tension between the high-flown and the humdrum, is what makes Thomas 'revolutionary'. So 'spectacular in being unspectacular', so 'revolutionary because they lack the exaggeration of rhetoric', are the poems of Bishop and Thomas that these two poets now occupy major rather than minor, dominant rather than diminished, positions in the history of twentieth-century poetry, displacing some of the more grandiloquent and garish cocks of the walk of their respective eras – Robert Bridges, say, or Robert Lowell – by dint of having looked long and hard:

At four o'clock
in the gun-metal blue dark
we hear the first crow of the first cock

just below
the gun-metal blue window
and immediately there is an echo

off in the distance,
then one from the backyard fence,
then one, with horrible insistence,

grates like a wet match
from the broccoli patch,
flares, and all over town begins to catch.

Elizabeth Bishop's long, hard look at 'Roosters', with their 'horrible insistence', is a poem, and a phrase, Marianne Moore must have had in mind when she wrote, in the same 1946 *Nation* review I quoted earlier:

> With poetry as with homiletics, tentativeness can be more positive than positiveness; and in *North & South*, a much instructed persuasiveness is emphasized by uninsistence.

The word 'insistent' also occurs, in the phrase 'insistent buttonholers', in Bishop's own 1941 prose piece 'Mercedes Hospital'. It 'was because of Marianne Moore', as Bishop acknowledges in 'Efforts of Affection', 'that in 1935 my poems first appeared in a book'. Her 'older mentor' is more likely than not to have had the opportunity to read, and have her own critical terminology influenced by, the description in 'Mercedes Hospital' of a certain Miss Mamie:

> Above all, there is her inquisitiveness and talkativeness and that childlike expression in her eyes when she takes hold of my shoulders and peers into my face and asks question after question – just as St. Anthony might have rushed out of his cell, and seized a traveler by the elbow and naïvely but determinedly asked him for news of the world. In fact, all the saints must have been insistent buttonholers, like Miss Mamie.

Let me go back now to the opening paragraph/stanza of '12 O'Clock News' ('of the world'), and the opening phrase, which I described earlier as being 'at once buttonholing and blasé':

> As you all know, tonight is the night of the full moon, half the world over.

It's only by the time we get to the second phrase, 'tonight is the night of the full moon', that we understand that the '12 O'Clock' referred to is midnight rather than noon, the time when writers 'burn the midnight oil', an activity which sometimes leads their work to 'smell of the lamp', as '12 O'Clock News' will – wittingly so, I believe – using vocabulary such as 'glacis', 'calcareous', *'numen'* and 'indigenes'. Only by the time we reach the word 'moon' do we connect the italicized caption on the left with the text on the right, only on that word does what we ordinarily think of as a metaphor come into existence:

> The word 'metaphor' is just a highfalutin description of a very common, ubiquitous process by which all of us try to increase our understanding of the world around us. You move from the familiar to the unfamiliar. You use what you know as a tool for trying to better understand what you don't know.

That, believe it or not, was Vice President Al Gore, quoted on the subject of metaphor in a profile in *The New Yorker* of 31 July 2000. According to my other favourite bathroom reading, *The New Princeton Handbook of Poetic Terms* (or, if I'm expecting to stay for a while, *The New Princeton Encyclopedia of Poetic Terms*), the term 'metaphor' means 'transference':

> Metaphor is a trope, or figurative expression, in which a word or phrase is shifted from its normal uses to a context where it evokes new meanings. When the ordinary meaning of the word is at odds with the context, we tend to seek relevant features of the word and the situation that will reveal the intended meaning ... Following I.A. Richards, we can call a word or phrase that seems anomalous the 'vehicle' of the trope and refer to the underlying idea that it seems to designate as the 'tenor'.

I'm afraid I never fail, when I hear these terms, to think of that dreadful old shaggy-dog story which ends with the line about the tenor being Pavarotti, the vehicle a stretch limousine. That's partly, I suspect, because I've never been able to get the terms straight in my mind and, if I ever do, find them less than revelatory, simply because in many poems it's not entirely clear if Pavarotti's carrying the limo or the limo's carrying him. That uncertainty is thrown into sharp relief by '12 O'Clock News', where the basic elements of the metaphors are at once joined and disjoined, the engine simultaneously souped up, supercharged, and stripped down, spread out all over the front lawn. The conventional reading of the metaphors in '12 O'Clock News' would propose that the 'tenor' is, in each instance, what we find in the italicized left-hand column, the 'underlying idea' of the '*ashtray*', say, while the 'vehicle', the idea that seems anomalous – 'the nest of soldiers' who 'lie heaped together' – appears on the right. Or is it the other way round? Isn't 'the nest of soldiers' who 'lie heaped together' as strong a contender for the status of 'underlying idea' or 'tenor', the '*ashtray*' as likely to be the 'vehicle', the 'idea that seems anomalous'? It depends very much on what one takes the 'subject' of '12 O'Clock News' to be. I've already suggested that the poem would seem to be most immediately 'about' a 'small, backward country' with an 'inscrutable people' who are our 'opponents' – in other words, a poem of political engagement, perhaps even a poem calling for political action. The very *in*action described in the opening sentences, whereby the '*gooseneck lamp*' is compared, feebly, to the feeble 'moon' (or the 'moon', feebly, to the feeble '*gooseneck lamp*'), is indicative of a sense of stagnancy and stasis that continues to hang over '12 O'Clock News'. This sense of being in some sort of doldrums suggests another part of the provenance of those italicized legends, a provenance encoded in the description of a 'moon' that is 'dead' and 'motionless':

> All in a hot and copper sky,
> The bloody sun, at noon,
> Right up above the mast did stand,
> No bigger than the Moon.
> Day after day, day after day,
> We stuck, nor breath nor motion;

As idle as a painted ship

Upon a painted ocean.

This is not to speak of the nod and wink of the term '*gooseneck*' in the direction of another large, seagoing bird yoked to another 'neck':

Ah! well a-day! what evil looks

Had I from old and young!

Instead of the cross, the Albatross

About my neck was hung.

Directly to the left of that last stanza of 'The Rime of the Ancient Mariner', in the exaggerated margin, Coleridge gives an 'argument', often rendered in an italic typeface, of the narrative:

The shipmates, in their sore distress, would fain throw the whole guilt on the ancient mariner: in sign whereof they hang the dead sea-bird round his neck.

Though there's a comic side to the fact that this prose 'argument', or précis, is made up of twenty-seven words, four more than the twenty-three of the verse stanza on which it comments, the very fact that the prose occupies a little more space in the world would seem to substantiate Coleridge's famous observation, recorded in *Table Talk*, that prose is made up of 'words in their best order', while poetry is made up of 'the *best* words in their best order'.

*

With Coleridge's less than helpful distinction in mind, let me try now to address the point at which '12 O'Clock News' stops being verse and becomes prose. It happens somewhere between the end of the third sentence and the beginning of the fourth, almost certainly between the words 'dead' and 'visibility'. Maybe there's a way of testing it. One may imagine, for example, a free-verse poem in which the first two lines read:

> As you all know, tonight is the night
> Of the full moon, half the world over.

There's an obvious break after 'night'. That way, the phrase 'of the full moon' may be withheld so that a discovery, admittedly modest, about the nature of the 'night' may be made as the reader rounds the corner. This first line has nine syllables and four uneven stresses, as does the second. The end of this second line coincides with the end of a unit of sense, 'half the world over'. The repetition of a nine-syllable, four-stress line establishes a pattern, a set of expectations which the poem, were it written in verse, might build upon, either concurring with or, from time to time, running counter to them. So far so good. Let's see how the next line might go, if we were attempting to take the present words in the present order and, as if such a thing were possible, convert them into lines of free verse. This third line might read as follows:

> But here the moon seems to hang

There'd be a very clever enjambment there as we were left hanging on 'hang', but the line seems a bit on the short side, with only seven syllables and three stresses. Let's try again:

> But here the moon seems to hang motionless

That allows another modest play on the mimesis of the line coming to rest on that key word 'motionless'. We've ten syllables, four stresses. Not bad. Either of these two lines would support the idea, which I mentioned earlier, that it's only with the word 'moon' that we begin to make sense of the *'gooseneck lamp'*. Having admired the justice of the comparison, we may now go back and understand the physical verifiability of the 'moon' and the *'gooseneck lamp'* lighting only 'half the world', a somewhat more engaging prospect than the basic 'moon'/*'gooseneck lamp'* nexus. The net is cast a little wider, and the note struck a little wittier, in this next sentence: 'It gives very little light; it could be dead.' Let's go back now to the business of 'translating' this 'prose poem' into verse:

But here the moon seems to hang motionless

might be followed up by

in the sky. It gives very little light; it could be dead.

So far, fairly good. But the halting effect of the sequence of three short (two- or three-stress) phrases combined in this sentence and the next brings the verse rhythm, such as the one I've been bold enough to impose, to just that: a halt. 'It gives very little light; it could be dead. Visibility is poor.' The 'dead' there refers to both the everyday description of a lightbulb that no longer functions and the barren, reflective surface of the moon. It also refers, *self*-reflectively, to the precise moment in this prose poem where there's an acknowledgment that the rhythms are indeed those of prose rather than verse, where it is, in terms of the verse structure, 'dead' in the water. It's a measure of Bishop's genius, as well as the 'endless labour' she alludes to in the *'typewriter'* section, that she allows the poem a further commentary on itself by following up the crucially positioned 'dead' with the crucially positioned 'visibility', announcing the central concern of the poem to be what I described earlier as 'looking long and hard', however adverse the conditions. After the lopped-off, fitful 'It gives very little light; it could be dead. Visibility is poor', comes the leisurely, fluent 'Nevertheless, we shall try to give you some idea of the lay of the land and the present situation.'

*

Let me concentrate for a moment on that phrase 'the lay of the land', which, redolent as it is of the double meaning of lay as 'lie' and 'a short lyric or narrative poem intended to be sung', might well be Elizabeth Bishop's motto. One need look no further than the titles of her books – *North & South*, *A Cold Spring*, *Questions of Travel*, *Geography III* – to see that topographical map-reading might be described as her major subject. The very first poem in her first book, *North & South*, is called 'The Map', and it shows her at her understated best:

> The names of seashore towns run out to sea,
> the names of cities cross the neighboring mountains
> —the printer here experiencing the same excitement
> as when emotion too far exceeds its cause.

Bishop follows up this intellectually engaging metaphor with an even more physically engaging one:

> These peninsulas take the water between thumb and finger
> like women feeling for the smoothness of yard-goods.

Not only is this metaphor engaging, it is beautifully gauged – in the sense that it's as finely measured as the process of fine measurement it describes. The idea of the gauge is related to the idea of scale, and the idea of scale, appropriate or inappropriate ('as when emotion too far exceeds its cause'), is central to any number of Bishop's poems. I think of 'At the Fishhouses', a poem that refers to 'scales' in another sense in its description of an old man:

> There are sequins on his vest and on his thumb.
> He has scraped the scales, the principal beauty,

from unnumbered fish with that black old knife,

the blade of which is almost worn away.

There's a reference to this secondary meaning of 'scales' in the *'typewriter'* paragraph/stanza of '12 O'Clock News', complete with a little fish, a carp, glinting there just under the surface of '*escarp*ment', an instance of subliminality vastly more probable than that supposedly presented in George W. Bush's recent television advert in which the word 'rats' appeared for a thirtieth of a second before filling out to become 'bureaucrats':

> The escarpment that rises abruptly from the central plain is in heavy shadow, but the elaborate terracing of its southern glacis gleams faintly in the dim light, like fish scales.

I think of 'Crusoe in England', with its reference to a 'scale' in yet another sense, where the speaker recalls how he 'made home-brew':

> I'd drink
> the awful, fizzy, stinging stuff
> that went straight to my head
> and play my home-made flute
> (I think it had the weirdest scale on earth)
> and, dizzy, whoop and dance among the goats.

In the case of both these poems, 'At the Fishhouses' and 'Crusoe in England', there's a subliminal connection between these 'scales', musical or fishy, and a scale in the sense of a 'graduated table' of relative largeness or smallness. In 'At the Fishhouses', the poem moves from a close-up of the 'sequins', through a medium shot of a seal described as being 'interested in music; / like me a believer in total immersion, / so I used to sing him Baptist hymns', to a wide shot of a sea:

It is like what we imagine knowledge to be:

dark, salt, clear, moving, utterly free,

drawn from the cold hard mouth

of the world, derived from the rocky breasts

forever, flowing and drawn, and since

our knowledge is historical, flowing, and flown.

This movement from the specifics of harvesting to a meditation on the big picture is reminiscent of Robert Frost's method in 'After Apple-Picking', from the echoes of Frost's 'long two-pointed ladder' in Bishop's 'steeply peaked roofs / and narrow, cleated gangplanks [that] slant up / to storerooms in the gables', of Frost's 'barrel' in Bishop's 'big fish tubs completely lined / with layers of beautiful herring scales', of Frost's 'ten thousand thousand fruit' in Bishop's 'unnumbered fish', of Frost's 'My instep arch not only keeps the ache, / It keeps the pressure of a ladder-round' in Bishop's 'If you should dip your hand in, / your wrist would ache immediately, your bones would begin to ache', its allusive aspect underlined by the repetition, lest we miss it first time around. 'Crusoe in England' has a Frostian allusion, also, one which is already hinted at in that image in 'At the Fishhouses' of the 'black old knife' used to scrape the scales, whereby Crusoe's knife is an artefact emblematic of art:

The knife there on the shelf –

it reeked of meaning, like a crucifix.

It lived. How many years did I

beg it, implore it, not to break?

I knew each nick and scratch by heart,

the bluish blade, the broken tip,

the lines of wood-grain on the handle ...

This last line refers to Frost's celebrated description of 'The Ax-Helve' as poem:

He showed me that the lines of a good helve
Were native to the grain before the knife
Expressed them, and its curves were no false curves
Put on it from without. And there its strength lay
For the hard work.

The combination of aesthetics and erotics embodied by 'The Ax-Helve' are clear from subsequent descriptions of how the French-Canadian, Baptiste, 'chafed its long white body / from end to end with his rough hand shut round it'. It's Baptiste who comments, in the last line of the poem, 'See how she's cock her head!' A few lines earlier, the ax-helve is described as follows:

Erect, but not without its waves, as when
The snake stood up for evil in the garden –

There's a similar connection of a tool connected with writing, as the ax-helve most certainly is, in the '*typewriter eraser*' paragraph/stanza of '12 O'Clock News':

At last! One of the elusive natives has been spotted! He appears to be — rather, to have been — a unicyclist-courier, who may have met his end by falling from the height of the escarpment because of the deceptive illumination. Alive, he would have been small, but undoubtedly proud and erect, with the thick, bristling black hair typical of the indigenes.

This is a wonderful instance, I think, of Bishop's trademark tendency towards the corrective phrase ' — rather, to have been — ', particularly when it's mimetic, once again, of the activity it describes, that of 'correction' by 'erasure'. This sense of Bishop's poems being made up of erasure upon erasure, blank upon blank, reminds me of Robert Lowell's evocation of her work methods in 'Calling':

Do

you still hang your words in air, ten years

unfinished, glued to your notice board, with gaps

or empties for the unimaginable phrase –

There's now something faintly unimaginable, given our politically correct era, about the phrase 'with the thick, bristling black hair typical of the indigenes'. Even as far back as the early to mid 1970s, it would surely have raised a question about the attitude of the speaker, particularly when read in conjunction with the description in the '*ashtray*' paragraph/stanza of 'the childishness and hopeless impracticality of this inscrutable people, our opponents'. Even then, it would have been difficult to read such descriptions without questioning whether or not they were meant to be taken at face value, if it might not be necessary to read them as being ironized. The term 'inscrutable', for example, now has a racist tinge to it when used straight-facedly of anyone of Asian background. As I suggested earlier, the Asians who would have come most immediately to mind as 'our opponents' in the early to mid 1970s would have been the North Vietnamese, this group 'in hideously contorted positions, all dead' familiar from the daily news, or from the poems of Robert Lowell:

'It was at My Lai or Sonmy or something,

it was this afternoon... We had these orders,

we had all night to think about it –

it was to burn and kill, then there'd be nothing

standing, women, children, babies, cows, cats...

As soon as we hopped the choppers, we started shooting.

I remember... as we was coming up upon one area

in Pinkville, a man with a gun... running – this lady...

Lieutenant LaGuerre said, "Shoot her." I said,

"You shoot her, I don't want to shoot no lady."

She had one foot in the door... When I turned her,
there was this little one-month-year-old baby
I thought was her gun. It kind of cracked me up.'

Now I don't suppose that anyone is about to suggest that the views expressed here are those of Robert Lowell. We have lots of indicators – the fact that the poem is within quotation marks, that the speech is so idiomatic and ungrammatical – that there's a continental divide between the content of the poem and the contention of the author. The same applies to '12 O'Clock News', though it may not be quite so obvious. However much we may recognize elements of the poem as being Bishopian – I want to say 'Episcopal' – the speaker of the poem is clearly not the archetypical Bishop speaker. No attempt is made here to synthesize the jostling modes of discourse I pointed to earlier – the modes of the anthropologist/sociologist, the travel writer, the foreign/war correspondent, the radio/television reporter. There is no attempt to synthesize the jangling imagery of a poem which appeals at one moment to the Vietnam War, at another to the Cold War, as in the *'ink-bottle'* stanza/paragraph:

The natural resources of the country being far from completely known to us, there is the possibility that this may be, or may contain, some powerful and terrifying "secret weapon."

There's a 'secret weapon' of sorts deployed here by Bishop herself, since the text set down by the pen dipped in this ink-bottle has a sub-text, one that's a lot more substantial than the cliché of 'the pen is mightier than the sword'. The tonal breaks in the surface of '12 O'Clock News' point to an underlying stress in the speaker, of whom it might be as truly be said as of the speaker in the Lowell poem that the subject-matter has 'kind of cracked [her] up'. This may not be so immediately recognizable here because of the playful aspect of the poem (I'm reminded that the term 'lay', in the 'poem' sense, is thought to be related to the

Latin word *ludus*), but the extreme circumstances of Bishop's speaker are no less convincing, or full of conviction, than Lowell's. It's difficult not to see a certain passion and pity in Bishop's description of the soldiers 'heaped together in hideously contorted positions'. I write 'soldiers', though I may mean 'cigarette butts'. The confusion is similar to the one which Bishop raises in 'Poem', as the poem immediately following '12 O'Clock News' is tellingly entitled:

> A specklike bird is flying to the left.
> Or is it a flyspeck looking like a bird?

In any event, I come away with a sense of Bishop's own pain from one particular detail in this section, that of the white cigarette papers being reminiscent of 'uniforms ... designed to be used in guerrilla warfare on the country's one snow-covered mountain peak'. The exposure of these 'soldiers' is emblematic of Bishop's own sense of exposure, I think, one which has a poignancy that's all the more evident when we consider the place of the cigarette in her poems and letters. In 'At the Fishhouses', for example, the speaker and the old man with 'the sequins on his vest and his thumb' is emotionally connected to the speaker when he 'accepts a Lucky Strike' from her. In 'A Cold Spring', 'Greenish-white dogwood infiltrated the wood, / each petal burned, apparently, by a cigarette-butt'. In a letter written while she was an undergraduate at Vassar she reports:

> It is a wonderful cold night here. I live up in a tower (that isn't a figure of speech) and so have a fine view of the stars and the smokestacks of the power plant. A ladder goes up out of our living room or lobby onto the roof and once up among the elaborate Victorian iron railings, it's a very nice spot to smoke a dishonest cigarette. We are gradually filling the gutters with butts.

This positioning of the writer of the Vassar letter ('I live up in a tower ... and so have a fine view') is echoed by the speaker of the '*ashtray*' paragraph/ stanza:

> From our superior vantage point, we can clearly see into a sort of dugout, possibly a shell crater, a 'nest' of soldiers.

There's a complex psychodrama underlying these lines. The representation of the male organ as 'proud and erect, with the thick bristling black hair' in the '*typewriter eraser*' paragraph/stanza is followed here by a representation of the female organ as 'a sort of dugout, possibly a shell crater, a "nest"'. Several of these images are familiar to us from other Bishop poems, including this last 'nest', recognizable from 'Jeronimo's House', the poem immediately preceding 'Roosters' in *North & South*, in which 'my house' is described as 'my gray wasp's nest / of chewed-up paper / glued with spit' and 'my love-nest':

> At night you'd think
> my house abandoned.
> Come closer. You
> can see and hear
> the writing-paper
> lines of light

The connection between 'the writing-paper' and 'lines of light' is an exact prefiguring of the method of '12 O'Clock News'. The words 'dugout' and 'crater' point us back in the direction of 'Crusoe in England'. Now, the first of these, 'dugout', doesn't actually appear in the poem, nor indeed in *Robinson Crusoe*, but Crusoe's intellectual failure in making what, after the early nineteenth century, would be known as a dugout, in the 'canoe' sense, so far from the water, is surely one of the most revealing episodes in Defoe's novel, revealing both of Crusoe's resolve and resignation:

This grieved me heartily, and now I saw, tho' too late, the folly of beginning a work before we count the cost, and before we judge rightly of our own strength to go through with it.

Happily, the word 'crater(s)' does appear in 'Crusoe in England', in connection with the 'volcanoes', of which there are 'fifty-two' on the island, 'volcanoes dead as ash-heaps'. The *'ashtray'* paragraph/stanza, with its panoramic view of the 'dead' soldiers, sends me to that other sense of the term 'dead soldiers' – to which Lowell surely refers, perhaps unconsciously, in his use of the word 'empties' to describe 'the gaps ... for the unimaginable phrase' for which Bishop might wait for 'ten years'. There's no mention in '12 O'Clock News' of the empty 'drink-bottle' – as likely, alas, to have been a fixture of Bishop's desk as the *'ink-bottle'* we do find here. The fact that a 'bottle of ink' was one of the few items Defoe's Crusoe 'would have given it all for' makes me want to try to substantiate my sense of the 'complex psychodrama', as I described it, underlying not only these lines about the '"nest" of soldiers' but the earlier assertion, in the *'pile of mss.'* stanza/paragraph, that 'There are believed to have been no casualties'. Yet again, the surface jauntiness of this phrase belies the subterranean disjuncture, whereby the speaker of the poem is, in a profound sense, a 'casualty', whereby the 'pain' and 'exposure' I associated earlier with the speaker is reminiscent of aspects of Bishop's own personal life, her alcoholism and her lesbianism, which were painful to her, or might have left her feeling exposed. Both these aspects of Bishop's life find their fairly obvious objective correlatives in the figure of Crusoe himself, Crusoe who'd 'drink / the awful fizzy, stinging stuff / that went straight to my head', Crusoe who writes of Friday:

> If only he had been a woman!
> I wanted to propagate my kind,
> and so did he, I think, poor boy.
> He'd pet the baby goats sometimes,

and race with them, or carry one around.

—Pretty to watch; he had a pretty body.

The single-sex nature of any possible relationship on Crusoe's island is echoed in the singularity of the other things of the world which he catalogues (that urge to itemize and tally of which Defoe's Crusoe is a master is carried over into the itemizing of both 'Crusoe in England' and '12 O'Clock News'), be it the singularity of the sun ('there was one of it and one of me'), the 'one kind of berry' used to make 'the awful, fizzy, stinging stuff', or the 'one tree snail, a bright violet-blue / with a thin shell' which 'crept over everything, / over the one variety of tree'. This snail reminds us of another sense of 'scale' connected in Bishop's mind with the 'graduated table' I touched on earlier, the extension of the fish-scale sense of 'one of the small thin membranous or horny outgrowths or modifications of the skin' to 'any of the thin pieces of metal composing scale-armour', a protection against the sense of exposure in the '*ashtray*' paragraph/stanza.

The relationship between this sense of 'scale' as 'armour' and 'graduated table' is clear from several other Bishop poems, including the erotic prose poem 'Rainy Season; Sub-Tropics'. In the 'Giant Snail' section of that poem, for example, the snail-speaker describes her shell as having a 'curled white lip' and its 'inside' being 'smooth as silk', but complains 'O! I am too big. I feel it. Pity me.' That combination of inappropriate emotional and physical scale is found once again in 'Crusoe in England' with its 'I often gave way to self-pity' and 'if I had become a giant, / I couldn't bear to think what size / the goats and turtles were', and in '12 O'Clock News' with its 'signboards on a truly gigantic scale', its pity for the dead 'soldiers' and, as I read it, a faint sense of 'self-pity' associated with alcoholism and other addictive behaviours. In another section of 'Rainy Season; Sub-Tropics' entitled 'Strayed Crab', the crab-speaker describes itself with astonishing directness as being 'the color of wine', sending this reader back immediately to that other, obsolete sense of the word 'scale', the very first listed in the *OED*, the sense of 'a drinking bowl or cup'. This 'Strayed Crab', who favours 'the oblique, the indirect approach, and I keep my feelings to myself', describes a nearby toad as being 'at least four times my size and yet so vulnerable'. We've already met this 'Giant Toad' in the first section of 'Rainy Season; Sub-Tropics', in which the toad-speaker prefigures the line used later by the 'Giant Snail', 'I am too big, too big by far. Pity me.' This 'Giant Toad' connects once more with '12 O'Clock News' in that other addictive thing of the world, the cigarette:

> Once, some naughty children picked me up, me and my two brothers. They set us down again somewhere and in our mouths they put lit cigarettes. We could not help but smoke them, to the end. I thought it was the death of me, but when I was entirely filled with smoke, when my slack mouth was burning, and all my tripes were hot and dry, they let us go. But I was sick for days.

I'll quote without comment a letter written by Bishop in November 1948 to her friend Carley Dawson:

> I don't know how to begin this letter or what to say or how to say it – but I guess the only thing to do is to take the plunge & get it over with... I got to feeling sorry for myself (why, I haven't the slightest idea) at your house on Saturday (this spell had been coming on for two or three weeks, I think) & drank up all your liquor & made myself good & sick & finally got myself (under my own steam) off on Monday to a weird kind of convalescent home here.

In his 'Afterword' to *Becoming a Poet*, David Kalstone's first-rate study of Bishop, Moore and Lowell, James Merrill quotes Kalstone's 'working notes' for the chapter he didn't live long enough to finish:

The Real Problem for Bishop: How to turn the descriptive poem into a narrative – while keeping it descriptive in nature.

Something of this 'Real Problem' may be seen to underlie '12 O'Clock News', a poem of which Merrill goes on to write:

> The vast and ominous moonscape in '12 O'Clock News' is a view of the writer's desk. Her dexterity has never been more sinister than here.

Merrill's sense of the enervated evenhandedness of '12 O'Clock News' – which he described elsewhere as 'her saddest poem' – is telling. It's as if it were somehow balanced in the scales (another key sense of that key word), as if the effect of stasis I pointed to earlier on resulted, yet again, from the twinned or mirrored aspect of the prose poem, including its physical presence on the page. I'm struck in rereading 'The End of March', three poems along from '12 O'Clock News' in *Geography III*, by the twinning and mirroring of at least one significant fixture in the 'proto-dream-house, my crypto-dream-house' presented there:

> At night, a *grog à l'américaine*.
> I'd blaze it with a kitchen match
> and lovely diaphanous blue flame
> would waver, doubled in the window.

A few lines later, the speaker focuses on another fixture more familiar from '12 O'Clock News':

> A light to read by—perfect! But—impossible.

This, along with the evidence of a letter written by Bishop on 23 January 1979 to James Merrill, suggests that the desk in '12 O'Clock News' is set in a proto- or crypto-'dream-house':

> When I think about it, it seems to me I've rarely written anything of any
> value at the desk or in the room where I was supposed to be doing it –
> it's always in someone else's house, or in a bar, or standing up in the
> kitchen in the middle of the night.

That the desk, or at least one item on it, belongs in a dreamscape is clear
from Brett Millier's *Elizabeth Bishop: Life and the Memory of It*, another first-rate
account of Bishop's life and work, in which Millier notes that Bishop recorded a
dream in which she was 'sleeping on a giant typewriter'. Millier also quotes a letter from Bishop to Lowell dated 15 January 1948:

> The water looks like blue gas – the harbor is always a mess, here, junky
> little boats all piled up, some hung with sponges and bobbles and always
> a few half sunk or splintered up from the most recent hurricane – it
> reminds me a little of my desk.

Millier connects this to the description, in 'The Bight', of a harbour at Key West:

> Some of the little white boats are still piled up
> against each other, or lie on their sides, stove in,
> and not yet salvaged, if they ever will be, from the last bad storm,
> like torn-open, unanswered letters.
> The bight is littered with old correspondences.

In addition to her pointing out that these 'correspondences' correspond to
the '*Correspondances*' of Charles Baudelaire's poem of that title, in which
'L'homme y passe à travers des forêts de symboles', Millier might have pointed
to the carry-over of the 'correspondences' to the '*envelopes*' in '12 O'Clock News'.

I'll come back to Baudelaire shortly. First, though, I want to mention Millier's tantalizing note on '12 O'Clock News' in which she writes that this prose poem 'had been with [Bishop] in fragments of verse since her Vassar days'. I'm indebted to Brett Millier herself, and to Dean M. Rogers of the Special Collections of Vassar College Libraries, for so graciously putting me in the way of an uncollected poem dating as far back as 1950, early drafts of which are enti-tled both 'Desk at Night' and 'Little Exercise'. It's a poem which refers to 'a sort of landslide, / due, no doubt, to erosion of the soil' on which 'individual terrac-ings shine like scales'. We also find 'an exhausted unicyclist' with 'coarse black hair' who's 'fallen on the slope'. It's clear, by the way, from the drafts of '12 O'Clock News' itself, that Bishop's first instinct was to write 'slope' rather than 'glacis'. The definition of 'glacis' is revealing, though, since it refers specifically to the exposed area before a fortification, 'the parapet of the covered way extended in a long slope to meet the natural surface of the ground, so that every part of it shall be swept by the fire of the ramparts' (OED), substantiating a read-ing of the underlying tendency of this prose poem toward self-protection or self-defence. A word in a similarly obscure vein as 'glacis' which appears in a draft of '12 O'Clock News' is 'travertine', a reference to the shale found along the Tiber, replaced in the last version by 'calcareous', another sense of scale alluded to here being that of 'lime-scale'. The most intriguing note, for me, in the 'pile of mss.' relating to '12 O'Clock News', is the little multiplication sum in the mar-gin of the earliest page of notes which seems to read '25 x 4 = 100', perhaps a clue to the stanzaic pattern and number of lines of a possible version of the piece in verse. As we have it, the 1950 'Little Exercise/Desk at Night' poem refers to our familiar 'soldiers … in a machine-gun nest, / in the stained and wrinkled suits designed for camouflage in the snow' and to 'signboards … on a terrible scale'. The poem ends with the key image with which '12 O'Clock News' begins:

> At the top of the terraces, is it a cemetery?
> – illegible under a dead and goose-necked moon.

*

In my next lecture I'll be looking at 'I tried to think a lonelier Thing', a poem by that most desk-bound of poets, Emily Dickinson, whom Bishop described in an unpublished letter to Anne Stevenson, quoted by David Kalstone, as a 'self-caged bird'. I'll be attempting to determine the boundaries or borders between writer and reader, the extent to which the writer determines the role of the reader and, connected to that, the question of the location of the precise historical moment when we've been able to read an Emily Dickinson poem. In the meantime, I'll look very briefly at a few poems and at least one prose work related to the desk and its accoutrements in '12 O'Clock News'. The first is an influence *on* the prose poem, T.S. Eliot's 'Hysteria', which I mentioned at the outset. The speaker there describes an erotic encounter with a woman whose teeth, in an outlandish image reminiscent of some of the out-of-scale, militaristic images of '12 O'Clock News', are 'accidental stars with a talent for squad-drill'. At the centre of the poem is a desk of sorts, 'the rusty green iron table' on which a waiter is attempting to spread a pink and white checked cloth, while the woman laughs uncontrollably:

> I decided that if the shaking of her breasts could be stopped, some of the fragments of the afternoon might be collected, and I concentrated my attention with careful subtlety to that end.

The heavily ironized tone here feeds directly into the Bishop poem, just as the heavily ironized tone of a prose poem by Baudelaire, 'The Soup and the Clouds', feeds into the Eliot. In the Baudelaire piece, the speaker rhapsodizes on the beauty of his 'darling', as Michael Hamburger translates it, who is serving him dinner, only to be brought to his senses by her saying in a *'hysterical'* voice: 'Well, are you going to eat your soup or aren't you, you bloody dithering cloud-monger?' In his introduction to his translation of a selection of *Twenty Prose*

Poems, Hamburger suggests that 'the prose poem was a medium ... that enabled [Baudelaire] to illustrate a moral insight as briefly and as vividly as possible. Being an artist and a sensualist, he needed a medium that was not epigrammatic or aphoristic, but allowed him scope for fantasy and for that element of vagueness or suggestiveness which he considered essential to beauty.' Though Bishop was familiar with Baudelaire in French and, as we've seen, alludes to him in 'The Bight' both indirectly and directly ('if one were Baudelaire'), she was even more familiar with Baudelaire's great influence, Edgar Allan Poe, who determined Baudelaire's sense of the prose poem, some would argue, to a much greater degree than Baudelaire's fellow countrymen Maurice de Guerin and Aloysius Bertrand and Arsène Houssaye. As she explained in a 5 May 1938 letter to Marianne Moore, Bishop had set out quite deliberately to write a story 'according to a *theory* I've been thinking up down here out of a combination of Poe's theories and reading 17th-century prose!'. On May 2nd she'd written to Frani Blough to describe how she'd been 'doing nothing much but reread Poe' and evolving what she describes as a '"proliferal" style'.

That same style, based on the notion of 'the formation or development of cells by budding or division', might be said to have been at the heart of her work, including '12 O'Clock News', this prose poem collected in 1976 but first published much earlier, in *The New Yorker* of 4 March 1973. I mention the date only because it precedes by a decent interval the publication in 1975 of *Stations*, a series of prose poems by Seamus Heaney, a writer already influenced by Bishop's combination of tact and tactility. Heaney's 1972 collection *Wintering Out* had included 'Tinder', in which the lines 'We picked flints, / Pale and dirt-veined, / So small finger and thumb / Ached around them' would seem to derive from that image I quoted from Bishop's 'The Map' of 'These peninsulas take the water between thumb and finger / like women feeling for the smoothness of yard-goods'. In another poem in *Wintering Out*, 'Limbo', a woman is described as drowning her infant 'Till the frozen knobs of her wrists / Were dead as the gravel', while the last image describes how 'Even Christ's palms, unhealed, /

Smart and cannot fish there'. These last images are drawn, I suggest, from that description in 'At the Fishhouses' where 'If you should dip your hand in, / your wrist would ache immediately'. While the prose poems in *Stations* are most immediately influenced by Geoffrey Hill's *Mercian Hymns*, many of these 'trial runs across a territory' share a sense of the grand scale, the bird's-eye view, of Bishop's '12 O'Clock News', and the method of scrupulous observation followed by even more scrupulous observation:

> The drumming started in the cool of the evening, as if the dome of air were lightly hailed on. But no. The drumming murmured from beneath that drum. The drumming didn't murmur, rather hammered.

That prose poem ends with 'The air grew dark, cloud-barred, a butcher's apron', an image sufficiently outlandish to count as Martian, the term used of the work of Craig Raine, who has his own distinctive take on a butcher in the first poem in his 1978 collection *The Onion, Memory*:

> How the customers laugh! His striped apron
> gets as dirty as the mattress in a brothel ...
>
> At 10, he drinks his tea with the spoon held back,
> and the *Great Eastern* goes straight to the bottom.

While Raine has prepared the way for this last image by introducing the butcher as 'smoking a pencil like Isambard Kingdom Brunel', some of his readers experience the difficulty David Kalstone divined as 'The Real Problem for Bishop: How to turn the descriptive poem into a narrative – while keeping it descriptive in nature'. As recently as a 15 September 2000 review in the *Times Literary Supplement*, Gerald Mangan writes:

Raine's early poems, with their aimless catalogues of unrelated similes, always reminded me of gleaming rows of kitchen utensils, designed for exhibition and not for use.

Despite the profound sense of inertia with which many readers come away from the typical poem by Craig Raine, he has, at his best, learned to mimic Bishop's method of presenting a stripped-down, startling metaphor, often involving an unexpected jump in scale, as in 'The boy turns to offer me / A miniature organ of cigarettes' ('Trout Farm') or 'the lighthouse stands / like a salt cellar by Magritte' ('The Meteorological Lighthouse at O—'). This last leads me to a poem by a second Irish poet influenced by Bishop's characteristic method. Derek Mahon's 'A Lighthouse in Maine' owes much to Bishop's blend of specificity and non-specificity, what Marianne Moore described as her 'uninsistence':

> It might be anywhere –
> Hokkaido, Mayo, Maine;
> But it is in Maine.
>
> You make a right
> Somewhere beyond Rockland,
> A left, a right,
>
> You turn a corner and
> There it is, shining
> In modest glory like
>
> The soul of Adonais.
> Out you get and
> Walk the rest of the way.

Elsewhere, 'A Garage in Co. Cork' appeals to Bishop's 'Filling Station', his 'mound of never-used cement' echoing her 'cement porch behind the pumps', her 'pumps' echoed in his image of 'a god … changing to petrol pumps … an old man and his wife'. In 'Achill', there are several possible references to '12 O'Clock News', including a comparison of the 'sun' to a 'pearl bulb' and the line 'I glance through a few thin pages and turn off the light'. In the *Key West* section of 'The Hudson Letter', we find not only an epigraph drawn from Bishop but a direct allusion to her as a 'shy perfectionist with her painter's eye' and the line, 'I keep on my desk here a coarse handful of Florida sea-moss'. In 'The Drawing Board' (as we must now think of the poem formerly titled 'Table Talk', with its nod in the direction of Coleridge), Mahon gives another version of the writer's desk in which the table does the talking:

> I pray for a wood-spirit to make me dance,
> To scare your pants off and upset your balance,
> Destroy the sedate poise with which you pour
> Forth your ephemeral stream of literature.

That 'poise' leads me to the 'anglepoise', as it appears in 'The Globe in North Carolina', where it 'Rears like a moon to shed its savage / Radiance on the desolate page'. It's one of these very lamps which features so prominently as a fixture on the desk of the narrator of Salman Rushdie's 1981 novel *Midnight's Children*, a novel about a critical moment in the history of a 'backward country', one which the narrator describes from a 'superior vantage point' while writing in an 'Anglepoised pool of light' – a version, I suggest, of the '*gooseneck lamp*' in '12 O'Clock News'. I'll end with another version of the lamp which appears in 'In Prison', the story Bishop was claiming in 1938 to have written in her 'proliferal' style based on Edgar Allan Poe and Sir Thomas Browne:

… the room I now occupy is papered with a not unattractive wallpaper, the pattern of which consists of silver stripes about an inch and a half wide running up and down, the same distance from each other. They are placed over, that is, they appear to be inside of, a free design of flowering vines which runs all over the wall against a faded brown background. Now at night, when the lamp is turned on, these silver stripes catch the light and glisten and seem to stand out a little, or rather, in a little, from the vines and flowers, apparently shutting them off from me.

Bishop follows this fastidious description with the very image she associates with Emily Dickinson:

I could almost imagine myself, if it would do any good, in a large silver bird cage! But that's a parody, a fantasy on my real hopes and ambitions.

This sense of being at once engaged and disengaged, which somehow hangs over '12 O'Clock News', is reinforced by two sentences from a 1972 letter to Louise Crane:

There's an Emily Dickinson room here in the Houghton Library – I've never had the courage to go and see it.

Notes on contributors

HARRY CLIFTON'S most recent book is *Berkeley's Telephone and Other Fictions*.

ELAINE GARVEY is a graduate of the M.Phil. course in creative writing at Trinity College, Dublin.

ADRIAN FRAZIER is Director of the M.A. in Drama and Theatre Arts in the English Department at the National University of Ireland, Galway. He is the author of *George Moore 1852–1933*.

MOLLY MCCLOSKEY is the author of *Solomon's Seal*, a collection of stories. *The Beautiful Changes* is forthcoming early next year.

TOM MAC INTYRE'S new play *The Gallant John-Joe* recently toured Ireland. 'The Highest Counter', published herein, is a chapter from a novel-in-progress.

PAUL MULDOON is Howard G.B. Clark Professor in the Humanities at Princeton University and Professor of Poetry at Oxford University. His *Poems 1968–1998* has just been published.

CONOR O'CALLAGHAN'S most recent collection of poems is *Seatown*.

RUTH PADEL'S latest book is *I'm a Man: Sex, Gods and Rock 'n' Roll*. Her next collection of poems, *Voodoo Shop*, and a selection from her 'Sunday Poem' columns in the *Independent on Sunday*, are forthcoming early next year.

PETER SIRR'S most recent collection of poems is *Bring Everything*.

GEORGE SZIRTES'S collected poems on Hungarian themes, *The Budapest File*, was published last year. *An English Apocalypse* will appear this autumn.